World Geography

Workbook

1 2 3 4 5 6 7 8 9 10
ISBN 0-8251-5674-2

J. Weston Walch, Publisher
P. O. Box 658 • Portland, Maine 04104-0658
walch.com
Printed in the United States of America

Table of Contents

Table of Contents, *continued*

Table of Contents, *continued*

To the Student

Welcome! This *Power Basics® World Geography Workbook* is designed to be used with your *Power Basics® World Geography* student text. Each activity will help reinforce, extend, or enrich the material in your textbook.

Reinforcement activities provide practice in what you have learned in the student text. These activities may be very similar to those in the textbook, or they may take a different approach to the content.

Extension activities include a number of different approaches to the material and may "extend" the information a bit further. They may include critical-thinking questions, research questions, or real-life applications. In some cases, information that is covered briefly in the text is developed further in the extension activities.

Since everyone learns in a different way, activities that invite the multiple intelligences are also included in this workbook. These activities help you connect to the material through approaches such as physical movement, partner and group dialogue and games, and visual respresentations.

Power Basics® is designed to give you the foundation you need to do well in school and beyond. This workbook builds on the material you have learned in the student text and gives you a solid skills base to help you meet your academic and other goals.

NAME:

UNIT 1 • ACTIVITY 1
What Is Geography?

Geography is a way of describing the special land and water features of the planet on which you live. There are five major themes of geography.

1. **Location** refers to the position of a specific place (absolute or relative).
2. **Place** is a specific area physically or culturally (the climate, people, vegetation, economic goods, history).
3. **Movement** talks about the transportation of people, ideas, and things.
4. **Human-environment interaction** refers to how people affect the world around them and how that world affects people.
5. **Region** is a group of places that have one or more similar characteristics, such as location, language, religion, and so on.

Read the following paragraph. Then write one example of each theme of geography that you found in the paragraph.

The fourteen-year-old girl woke up listening to her Japanese-made radio alarm clock. From her window, she could see that the sun was already rising behind the buildings in her city. She took a shower using water from the reservoir near her house. She put on her clothes, including a shirt made in Bangladesh and shoes made in Mexico. She headed down the stairs and into the kitchen. She poured herself some cereal made with grain grown in the U.S. Midwest, and added milk from the local dairy. She threw the empty milk jug into the recycling bin. She was looking forward to school today since there was going to be an assembly featuring all the international students. She had moved here from Russia a few years ago. She now lived in Boston, Massachusetts, near the Atlantic Ocean, and she felt right at home.

1. Location: ______________________________
2. Place: ______________________________
3. Movement: ______________________________
4. Human-Environment Interaction: ______________________________
5. Region: ______________________________

NAME:

UNIT 1 • ACTIVITY 2
Types of Maps

You use maps to understand geography. A globe is a more accurate way of drawing the world, because it is round like Earth itself. Since it is difficult to put a globe in your pocket, cartographers (mapmakers) have used a variety of map projections to show a round object on a flat surface.

Imagine an orange. Take the peel off, and try to flatten the peel. The areas around the outer edges appear stretched out. The same thing happens with maps, but they are still the best way to show different kinds of information about the world. Review the section on maps in your student text. Complete the crossword puzzle below.

Across

1. Use this type of map to see how much rain falls in an area.
5. Use this type of map to see how many people live in China.
6. Use this type of map to see where corn is grown and cattle are raised.

Down

1. Use this type of map to see where gold is found in Africa.
2. Use this type of map to find your way to a new friend's house.
3. Use this type of map to find a place that has cold temperatures year round.
4. Use this type of map to find the height of the Andes.
5. Use this type of map to see where paper is manufactured.

NAME:

UNIT 1 • ACTIVITY 3
Classroom Map

Create a map of your classroom in the space below. Include the following:

- **Title:** My Classroom
- **Author:** (your name)
- **Key:** Use color to indicate desks/tables, teachers' area, pencil sharpener, and other landmarks in the room.
- **Scale:** Use your feet. For example, if your room is 20 of your feet wide and your map is 20 inches big, then your scale will be 1" on your map = 1 ft. in the room.
- **Compass rose:** You will need to find out which direction is north, south, east, and west of your school.

NAME:

UNIT 1 • ACTIVITY 4
Continents and Oceans Game

In groups of four, use string or yarn to make the rough shapes of the continents in their correct locations on the floor. One student team will give the other team easy directions first. For example, "Travel from the biggest continent to the smallest." One student would stand on Asia and the other on Antarctica. If they get it correct (both the answer as well as the location), they are given a medium direction and then a hard direction. If they get all three correct, they get three points and the other team plays. Play proceeds back and forth, the winning team being the one that follows the most directions correctly. Teams may discuss answers before they step on their maps.

Directions

Easy

1. equator to Prime Meridian
2. Atlantic Ocean to Pacific Ocean
3. Indian Ocean to Arctic Ocean
4. Northern Hemisphere to Southern Hemisphere
5. Asia to Australia
6. Africa to South America
7. North America to Europe
8. Europe to Antarctica
9. Northern Hemisphere to Australia
10. Indian Ocean to South America

Medium

1. Latin America to North America
2. biggest continent to smallest continent
3. eastern Northern Hemisphere to western Southern Hemisphere
4. eastern Southern Hemisphere to eastern Northern Hemisphere
5. western Northern Hemisphere to eastern Southern Hemisphere
6. western Northern Hemisphere to western Southern Hemisphere
7. continent with the highest population to continent with the lowest population
8. Middle East to Southeast Asia
9. sub-Saharan Africa to Central America
10. Eastern Europe to the Middle East

Hard

1. driest continent with a permanent population to coldest continent
2. two continents that have the two longest rivers
3. two continents that have the two largest lakes
4. two continents with the highest mountains
5. the two deepest oceans
6. the two continents that each have about 13% of the world's population
7. equator to the Tropic of Cancer
8. equator to the Tropic of Capricorn
9. Prime Meridian to the International Date Line
10. any location in the world likely to lie on a fault line (movement of tectonic plates causing possible earthquakes or tsunamis)

NAME:

UNIT 1 • ACTIVITY 5
Latitude/Longitude

Place the following cities on the map as close as possible to their correct location using the latitude and longitude lines. Then answer the questions.

Washington, D.C., U.S.	38° N	77° W	Nairobi, Kenya	1° N	36° E
Quito, Ecuador	0°	78° W	Harare, Zimbabwe	17° S	31° E
Honolulu, HI, U.S.	21° N	157° W	Jerusalem, Israel	31° N	35° E
Punta Arenas, Chile	53° S	71° W	Novosibirsk, Russia	55° N	82° E
Greenwich, England, U.K.	51° N	0°	Perth, Australia	31° S	115° E

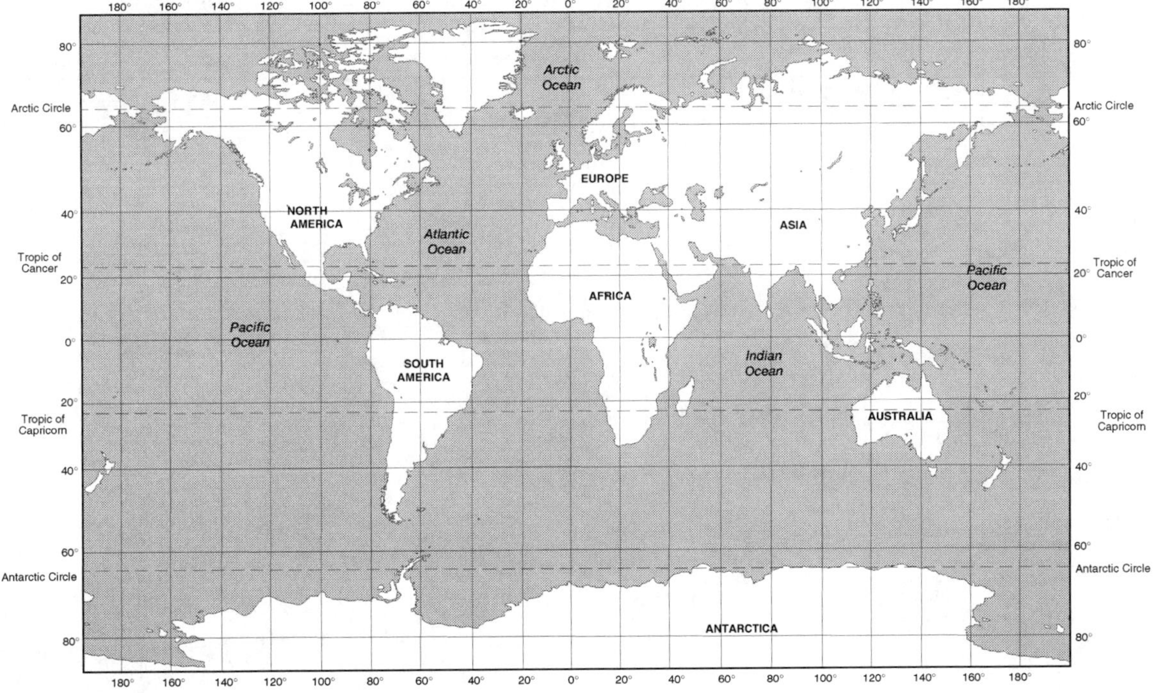

1. Name two of these cities that are on or near the equator. ______________________

____

2. Name the city that is on the Prime Meridian. ______________________

3. Name two cities in the Southern Hemisphere. ______________________

____

4. Name two cities in the Eastern Hemisphere.

____

NAME:

UNIT 1 • ACTIVITY 6
Create Your Own Island

Imagine that you have been exploring an uncharted part of the ocean. You and your team of scientists have discovered a new island. Now it is up to you to make sure it is mapped accurately.

Make a map of the new island in the space below.

- Include a title, a scale, and a compass rose on the map.
- Include the approximate latitude and longitude of your island. On the lines below the map, describe the island in relative location to the closest continents.
- On another sheet of paper, write a short story about your discovery. Include information about the climate, vegetation, and significant landforms of your island.

NAME:

UNIT 2 • ACTIVITY 7
Location: North America

Canada is often thought of as being north of the United States. For the most part, that is true. However, twenty-seven of the fifty U.S. states have land north of Canada's southernmost point, Middle Island, Ontario. These states are Alaska, California, Connecticut, Idaho, Illinois, Indiana, Iowa, Maine, Massachusetts, Michigan, Minnesota, Montana, Nebraska, Nevada, New York, New Hampshire, North Dakota, Ohio, Oregon, Pennsylvania, Rhode Island, South Dakota, Utah, Vermont, Washington, Wisconsin, and Wyoming.

Label the map below with only these 27 states. Note that Middle Island, Ontario, Canada, is already labeled for you. (*Note:* Because of the map projection, some states may not look as though they have land north of Middle Island.)

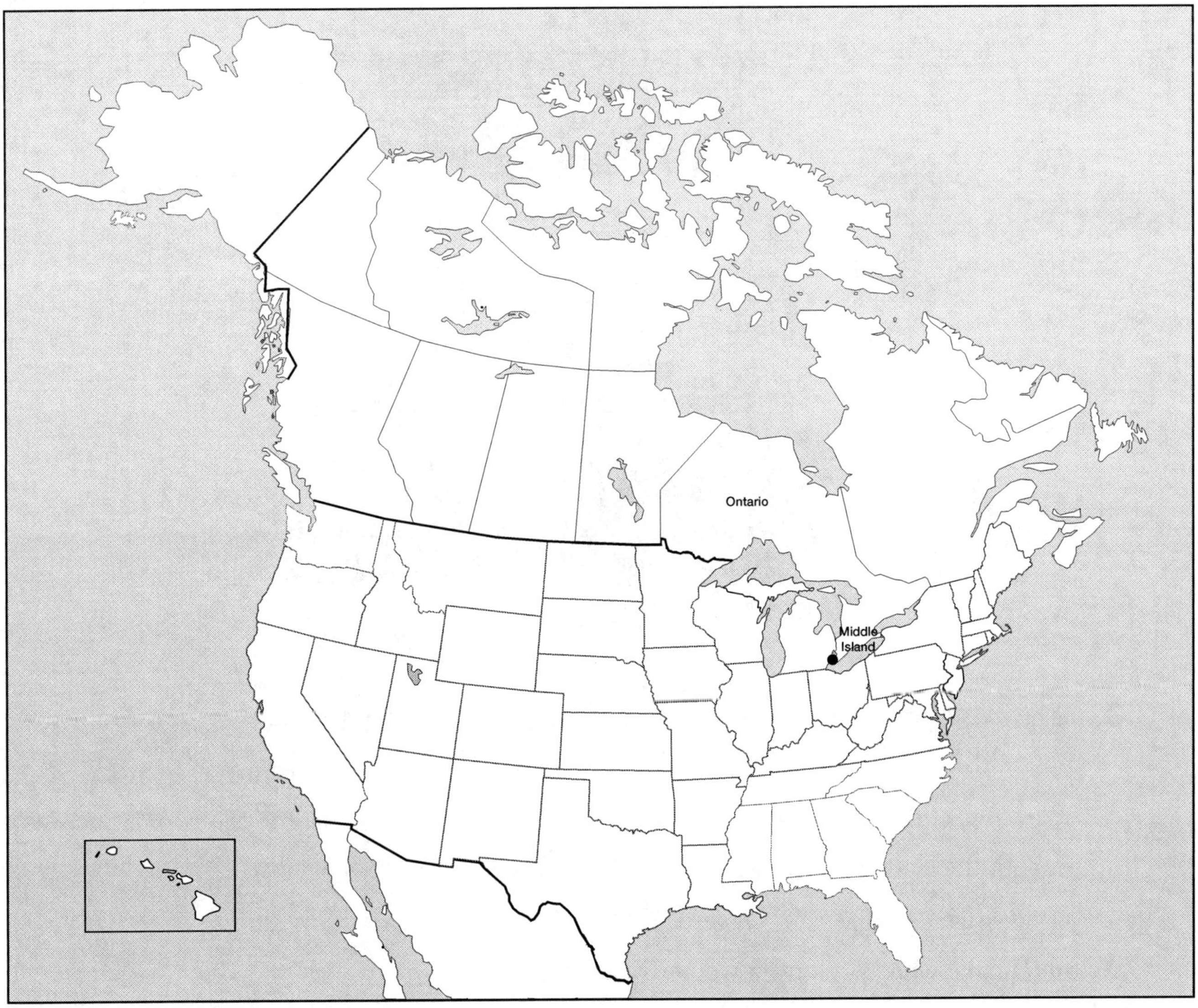

NAME:

UNIT 2 • ACTIVITY 8
Population in North America

Population pyramids show the percentages of males and females by age group in a particular country. The shape of the pyramid shows whether a population is growing or shrinking. Some countries have *rapid growth,* with half their population under the age of 20. This might be due to a high birthrate, war, or disease. Other countries have *negative growth,* meaning they might have a population that is mostly older due to war, emigration, or other reasons. Canada and the United States both have a *slow growth* pyramid structure. Using these graphs, people can predict long-term growth of a population.

Look at the two population pyramids below. Then answer the following questions.

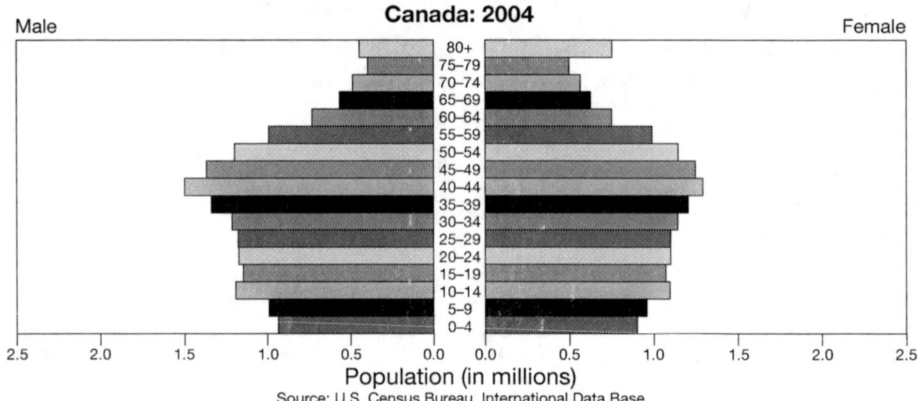

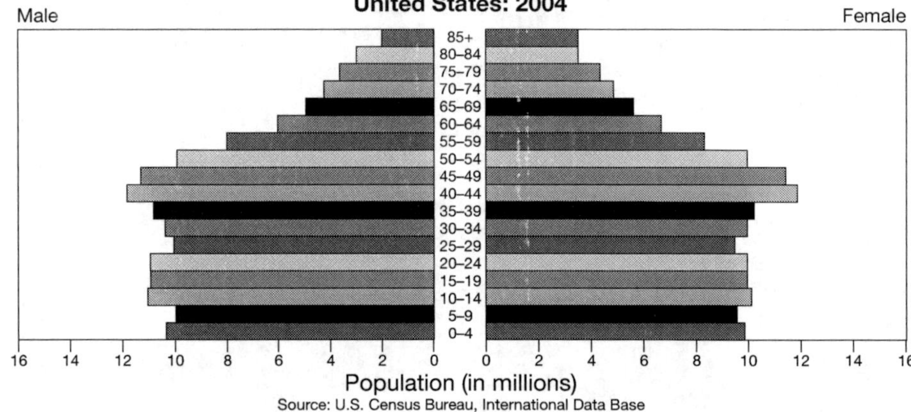

1. Which country, the United States or Canada, has a larger population, according to the two pyramids? ______________________

2. After World War II, there was a "baby boom" when a large segment of the population was born in both the United States and Canada. How old are these "babies" now? (*Name the three age groups that are largest on the graphs.*) ______________________

3. In Canada, who lives longer, women or men? ______________________

4. In the United States, approximately how many million people are under the age of 20?

____

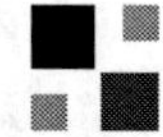

NAME:

UNIT 2 • ACTIVITY 9
Hawaii

Hawaii became the last state to join the union, in 1959. It had been settled by Polynesians 1,500 years earlier. It was first encountered by Europeans in 1778 when Captain James Cook arrived. Hawaii became a stopping point for traders and whalers. American settlers introduced a U.S.-style government. By 1839, there was a Declaration of Rights, and by 1840, a constitution and a legislature. Descendants of these American settlers profited from sugar plantations, an expanded shipping industry, and emerging pineapple plantations.

In 1893, sugar planters plotted to overthrow the local monarchy. They wanted to take over the islands for the United States to get rid of high tariffs. In 1898, Hawaii was annexed by the United States and became the Territory of Hawaii. The naval base at Pearl Harbor was established at the deep harbor in Honolulu. Pineapple plantations thrived. In 1900, there was a wave of immigrant laborers from Puerto Rico, Korea, and the Philippines. For the United States, World War II began after the bombing of Pearl Harbor on December 7, 1941. Then, in 1959, Hawaii became the 50th state. Hawaii is still a major military base for the United States, as well as an exporter of foods, such as pineapple and macadamia nuts. In the 1970s, tourism overtook the military as the main Hawaiian industry. Today, Hawaii makes almost a quarter of its entire income from tourism.

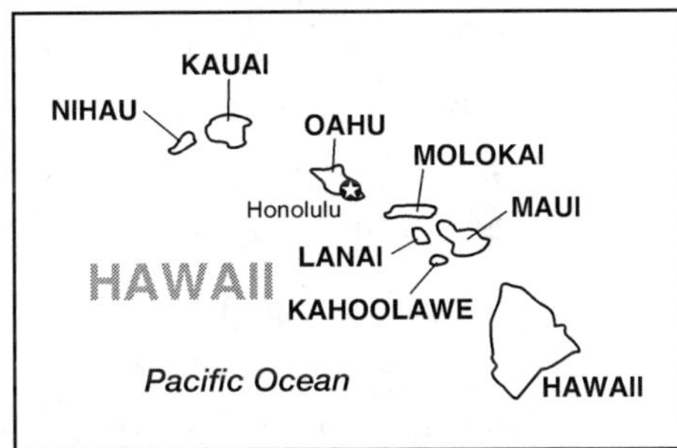

1. Imagine you are a tour guide in Honolulu, Hawaii. You want to attract people from all over the United States to your state. On the lines below, give at least one reason a person from each region would want to visit your state. You may wish to review in your text the climate and geography of each region, as well as the information on Hawaii above.

   New England ______________________________

   Mid-Atlantic States ______________________________

   South ______________________________

   Midwest ______________________________

   West ______________________________

   Pacific (other than Hawaii) ______________________________

2. How did the location of Hawaii make it a place fought over by the British, Russians, Americans, and French? (Think about economic resources as well as location.) Write your response on another sheet of paper.

NAME:

UNIT 2 • ACTIVITY 10
Nunavut

Imagine that during the month of June, you lived in a place that had 24 hours of sunlight every day! Or, in December, there was 24 hours of darkness every day. People who live in Nunavut experience just that. Canada created a third territory, Nunavut, in 1999. Meaning "our land," it is home to over 30,000 people, mostly Inuit. *Inuit* means "the people." Originally, Europeans called these people *Eskimos,* which was based on a Cree Indian word that meant "eaters of raw meat." This term is now considered an insult. Inuits are a people who live near the Arctic in Alaska, Canada, or Russia.

The territory of Nunavut covers one fifth of Canada and has a widely spread-out population. The territory is 1,900,000 square kilometers (roughly the size of Alaska, New York, Florida, and Massachusetts combined). The capital is Iqaluit and is located at 64° north latitude. (The Arctic Circle is at 67°!) Average January temperatures are –31°F. July temperatures average around 50°F. Nothing is accessible by road or rail. Airlifts and sealifts bring in all needed people, food, and supplies. For local trips, motorboats have replaced kayaks, and snowmobiles have made dog sledding a sport, rather than a necessity. Many people here work for the government, or in fishing, mining, or tourism.

Residents are able to retain a traditional way of life through hunting, fishing, and crafts. They also have access to modern health services and conveniences. There are several national parks where visitors can see polar bears, grizzly bears, caribou, musk-oxen, and much bird life, as well as spectacular scenery.

On another sheet of paper, write a letter to an Inuit person your age. In it, describe what you know about the Inuit territory. Compare it with your home in terms of climate, ease of shopping, and recreation. Include questions you have about his or her life. You may wish to use the Internet to find out more about Nunavut. Look at the Nunavut coat of arms and the flag to learn how these are symbolic of Inuit local culture.

NAME:

UNIT 2 • ACTIVITY 11
Coastal Waters of North America

North America is bordered by three oceans: the Pacific, Arctic, and Atlantic. In addition, there are many bays, channels, gulfs, islands, peninsulas, and straits along its coastlines.

Use the physical map of North America below to identify as many of these features as possible. Use six different colors to highlight the features listed below.

Color Key			
☐	Bay	☐	Island
☐	Channel	☐	Peninsula
☐	Gulf	☐	Strait

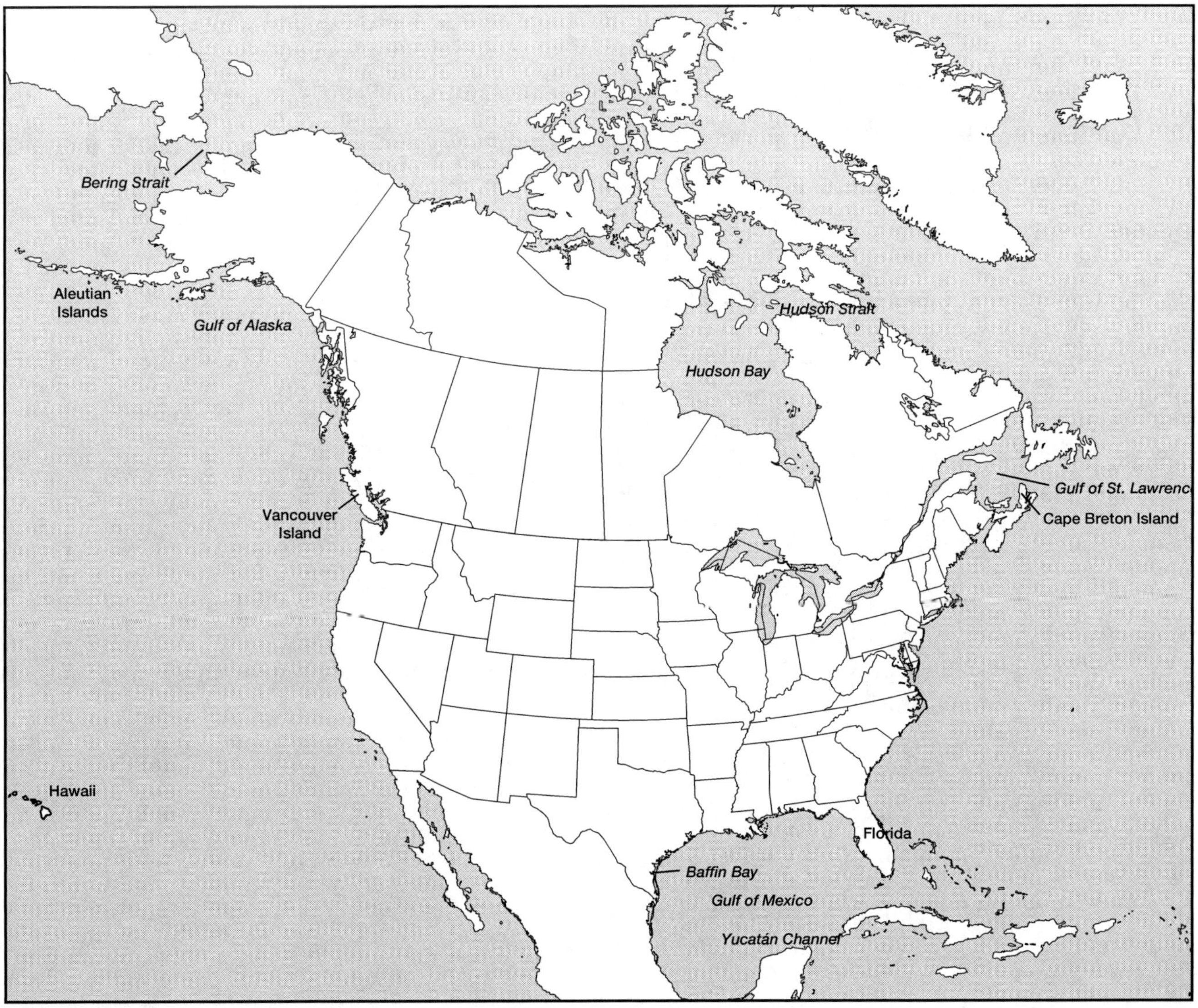

Bering Strait
Aleutian Islands
Gulf of Alaska
Hudson Strait
Hudson Bay
Gulf of St. Lawrence
Cape Breton Island
Vancouver Island
Hawaii
Florida
Baffin Bay
Gulf of Mexico
Yucatán Channel

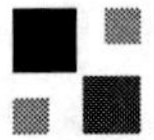

NAME:

UNIT 2 • ACTIVITY 12
The Mississippi River

The Mississippi River, from its source at Lake Itasca in Minnesota to the Gulf of Mexico, is 2,348 miles long. Cities along its banks, including Minneapolis, St. Paul, St. Louis, Memphis, and New Orleans, depend on the river for transportation, trade, and tourism.

Importance for Trade: Over 583 million tons of goods are transported through the Mississippi River Valley system each year. Wheat, soy, oil, and corn are just a few of the products carried along the river. The barge industry along the Mississippi is an important link between United States farming production and industry and global markets. According to a Mississippi River Museum exhibit, "One gallon of fuel can move one ton of grain 60 miles by truck, 200 miles by rail, and over 500 miles by water. Moving goods by water rather than by truck or rail helps reduce air pollution, traffic congestion, and wear and tear of the highways."

Impact of Natural and Human-made Disasters: The Mississippi River Flood of 1993 occurred when it rained too much in too many places. The flooding of the tributaries as well as the Mississippi River itself led to the river flooding six miles inland in some places. The impact on trade was disastrous because some of the river's locks had to be shut down. This kept ships from moving, and it stranded barges. An oil spill by a Nigerian heavy oil tanker on the lower Mississippi in 1998 closed a 28-mile stretch of the river for three days. This harmed the movement of local and international goods, and it damaged local ecosystems.

Answer the following questions.

1. Give three examples of why the Mississippi is good for business.

____

____

2. Predict three things that could happen that would harm the Mississippi River system.

____

____

3. Do further research on the Mississippi Flood of 1993. Then, on another sheet of paper, answer the following questions.
   - What is the definition of a flood?
   - Why did the flood occur?
   - How much area was affected by the flood?
   - What can be done to prevent future floods?

NAME:

UNIT 2 • ACTIVITY 13
North American Landforms

Use the clues to complete the crossword puzzle about landforms of the United States and Canada.

Across

3. The Sierra Nevada, in California, are called the ________________ Mountains in Canada.
6. This is the tallest mountain in North America.
7. Canadian Shield forests are called the ________________.
8. These are grasslands in the United States and Canada from which corn, wheat, soybeans, and livestock come.

Down

1. Both plains and plateaus are ________________.
2. These mountains in the western United States extend into Canada. They are called the Brooks Range in Alaska
4. This is a measurement above or below sea level.
5. The lowest part in North America is ________________ Valley.
6. The Appalachian mountain chain stretches from northern Georgia to ________________.

UNIT 2 • ACTIVITY 14
Introduction to Climographs

A climograph combines a line graph and a bar graph. It gives a picture of the climate of a particular place.

Look at the completed climograph below left for Banff. Precipitation is shaded in on the bar graph to show the inches of rain this location gets each month. Temperature is recorded by dots across the top part of the graph for each month. The climograph uses data from this table:

Banff, Alberta, Canada is at about 51° 10' N 115° 34' W.
Average Temperature and Precipitation

	Jan	Feb	Mar	Apr	May	Jun	Jul	Aug	Sep	Oct	Nov	Dec	Year
°F	12.4	18.3	25.7	36.7	45.5	52.2	57.9	55.9	47.8	39.2	25.0	16.5	35.8
inches	1.2	0.9	1.0	1.2	2.0	2.6	1.8	2.0	1.6	1.2	1.3	1.3	18.2

Now it is your turn. Use the data in the table for Miami to fill in the blank climograph below.

Miami, Florida is at about 25° 46' N 80° 11' W.
Average Temperature and Precipitation

	Jan	Feb	Mar	Apr	May	Jun	Jul	Aug	Sep	Oct	Nov	Dec	Year
°F	67.1	68.4	71.6	75.2	78.6	81.3	82.6	82.8	81.9	78.3	73.6	69.1	75.9
inches	2.0	2.1	2.5	3.2	5.9	9.0	6.0	7.8	8.5	7.0	3.1	1.9	59.0

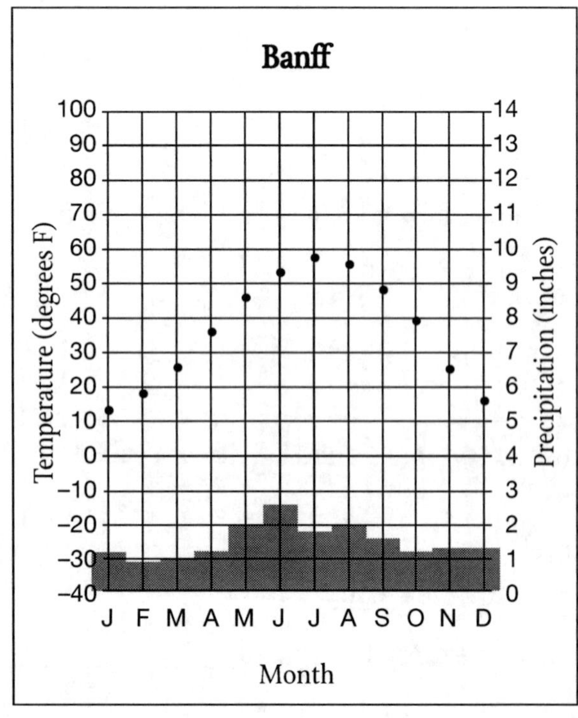

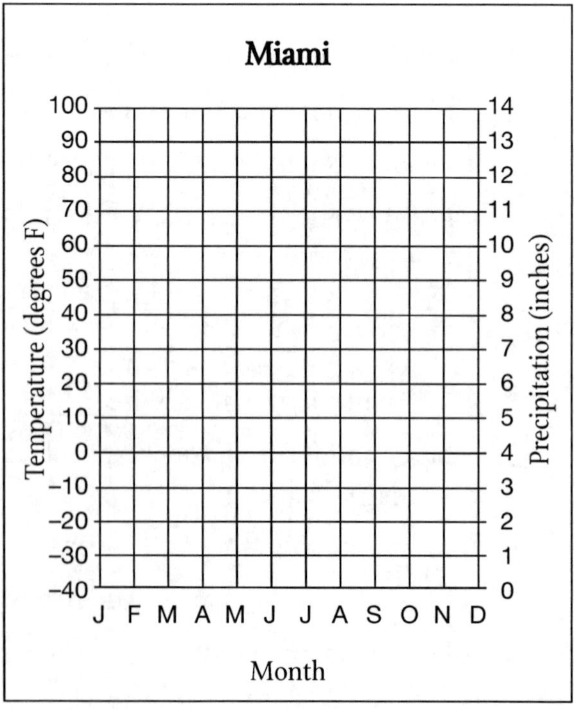

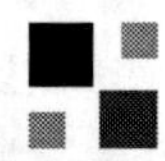

NAME: ______________________________

UNIT 2 • ACTIVITY 15
Agriculture: Wheat

Read the following paragraphs and study the chart. Then answer the questions.

Wheat is an important agricultural crop for both Canada and the United States. It was one of the first grains to be domesticated over 10,000 years ago. It was introduced to the Americas in the 1600s. Wheat does not require heavy irrigation, so it is often produced by using a dry farming method.

There are both winter and summer wheat varieties. Winter wheat is planted in milder areas where the threat of winterkill is reduced. It is planted in the fall and develops crowns and roots before freezing weather begins. With the first warm days of spring, wheat is ready to begin growing again. Winter wheat is harvested in late spring or early summer. Seventy-five percent of all wheat grown in the United States is winter wheat. In severe winter areas, winterkill is a big risk for many wheat varieties, so planting is in the spring. This wheat is called spring wheat, and it is harvested in the summer or fall. The Winter Wheat Belt centers on Nebraska, Kansas, and parts of Colorado, Wyoming, and Utah. Spring Wheat Belts are found on the Canadian Prairie, North Dakota, parts of South Dakota, and Montana. Kansas is first in wheat production, and North Dakota is usually second.

Wheat Statistics

	Canada	United States
Population	31,147,000	278,357,000
Arable land	45,560	176,950
Irrigated land	720	22,400
Wheat production (tons)	26,804,100	60,512,000
Harvested area (hectares)	10,962,900	21,460,000
Yield (kg/hectare)	2,445	2,819
Export (tons)	18,771,740	27,830,150

Source: www.fao.org Food and Agricultural Organization Statistics on American wheat-producing countries.

1. What is the difference between spring and winter wheat? ______________________________

   ____

2. Is most Canadian wheat likely to be winter wheat or spring wheat? ______________________________

3. Write three questions about wheat production in North America using the statistics in this chart. ______________________________

   ____

   ____

NAME:

UNIT 2 • ACTIVITY 16
Natural Resource Marketing Campaign

The United States and Canada are rich in natural resources. Coal is found in the Ohio River Valley. Petroleum and natural gas are present along the Gulf Coast and in California and Alaska. Copper, lead, and uranium are found in both the American and Canadian Rockies. The Canadian Shield is also a rich source of iron, zinc, and uranium.

Work in small groups for this activity. Choose one of the following regions: the Ohio River Valley, the Gulf Coast, California, Alaska, the Canadian Rockies, the Rocky Mountains, or the Canadian Shield. As a group, design an advertisement for a new industry to begin mining or drilling in one of these natural resource regions. Your advertisement should have a slogan to attract business to your region. You should include a picture of the resource, your region, or the local environment. You can use the Internet or encyclopedias to find pictures of these natural resources. In the space below, brainstorm ideas. Then complete your group project on another sheet of paper.

Region: ______________________________

Slogan: ______________________________

____

Ideas: ______________________________

____

____

____

____

____

____

____

____

____

____

____

____

____

____

NAME:

UNIT 2 • ACTIVITY 17
Urban Centers: United States and Canada

Use this chart to answer the questions that follow.

City	Population 2000	Location	Important Trade
New York City	8,008,278	large port on Atlantic Ocean	world leader in finance, the arts, fashion, and communications; tourism
Philadelphia	1,517,550	major transportation center (shipping—port and rail)	manufacturing, printing and publishing, health insurance, legal services, architecture, engineering, tourism
Boston	589,141	large port with harbor on Atlantic ocean	high-tech, financial, insurance, real estate, health care, educational hub; tourism
Chicago	2,896,016	major Great Lakes port	commercial, financial, industrial, cultural center of Midwest; agricultural commodities
Toronto	2,481,494	port of entry	commercial, financial, publishing, and industrial (including aircraft) hub; Canada's banking and stock-exchange center
Milwaukee	596,974	one of the largest Great Lakes ports	industrial center, printing, manufacturing, malt beverages (beer), iron and steel forgings, robotics
Cleveland	478,403	important port	corporate center for transportation, insurance, retailing, banking, finance
Ottawa	774,072	capital of Canada	telecommunications, microelectronics, photonics, software, life sciences, government, tourism
Montreal	1,039,534	excellent harbor on St. Lawrence Seaway	tourism, shipping, industrial and financial service center; pharmaceuticals, high-tech
Houston	1,953,631	large port on Gulf of Mexico	major business, financial, science, technology center; oil and natural gas; health-care services; aerospace
Los Angeles	3,694,820	large ports on the Pacific	major hub of shipping, manufacturing, industry, finance, entertainment; aerospace
San Diego	1,223,400	commercial port on Pacific	U.S. military contracts, medical and scientific research, oceanography, agriculture, tourism

On another sheet of paper, answer the following questions based on the chart above.

1. Name the top five cities in the United States in terms of population.
2. What is the most heavily populated Canadian city? Where does it rank in size with the American cities?
3. How many of the cities in the list are major port cities?
4. Give four comparisons among these cities based on the types of industries or trade for which they are known.

NAME:

UNIT 2 • ACTIVITY 18
Location: Latin America

Using your text as a reference, complete this dialogue between you and a student from Latin America.

Latin American student: So you want to know more about Latin America?

You: Yes. I need to know more for a school research project. So where exactly is Latin America?

Latin American student: Latin America includes everything south of the Rio Grande River—that means **1.** ______________________________.

You: Wow, that means Latin America is located in the western part of the world, but some countries are located in the Northern and some in the Southern **2.** ____________________.

Latin American student: The **3.** ____________________ cuts through the northern part of South America, through the country of Ecuador.

You: But then much of South America is south of the equator. Does that mean people in Argentina can go skiing in August?

Latin American student: That is true. In many Latin American countries, it is winter in South America when it is **4.** ____________________ in North America, since the Northern Hemisphere is tilted toward the **5.** ____________________ during June, July, and August.

You: I should come visit during my summer vacation so I can go snowboarding! What language should I learn to speak before I come? Latin?

Latin American student: Latin is a dead language, actually. Many languages are spoken in Latin America including **6.** ____________________, Portuguese, and French. All of these languages are called Latin languages, because they originate from Latin. Many people speak English, too. Also, some indigenous people still speak their language.

You: So does everyone live in what is left of the rain forest?

Latin American student: No, very few people live in the tropical interior. But you are correct that the rain forest is shrinking. Most Latin Americans live in coastal cities, just like North Americans.

You: What are some of the names of those coastal cities?

Latin American student: 7. ______________________________

You: I really do like to snowboard. Are there many mountainous regions in Latin America?

Latin American student: Many Latin American countries have highland areas. The Andes Mountain chain covers the whole western edge of the continent—there is some great snowboarding there!

You: What are some of these highland cities I might be able to visit?

Latin American student: 8. ____________________

You: Great! I have one more question . . . . **9.** ______________________________

____

Latin American student: 10. ______________________________

You: Thanks for talking with me!

UNIT 2 • ACTIVITY 19
Population Distribution in Haiti

The shape of a population pyramid shows whether a population is growing or shrinking. There are some countries that have slow growth rates. A slow growth pyramid would look somewhat like a square since the population growth is nearly constant. Other countries have negative growth, meaning that they have a population that is mostly older, due to war, emigration, or other reason. Many countries in Latin America are experiencing rapid growth rates, where half of the population is under the age of 20. This might be due to a high birthrate, war, or disease. These pyramids tend to be triangular in shape.

Look at the population pyramid for Haiti, and answer the questions that follow. Pay close attention to the population number in millions.

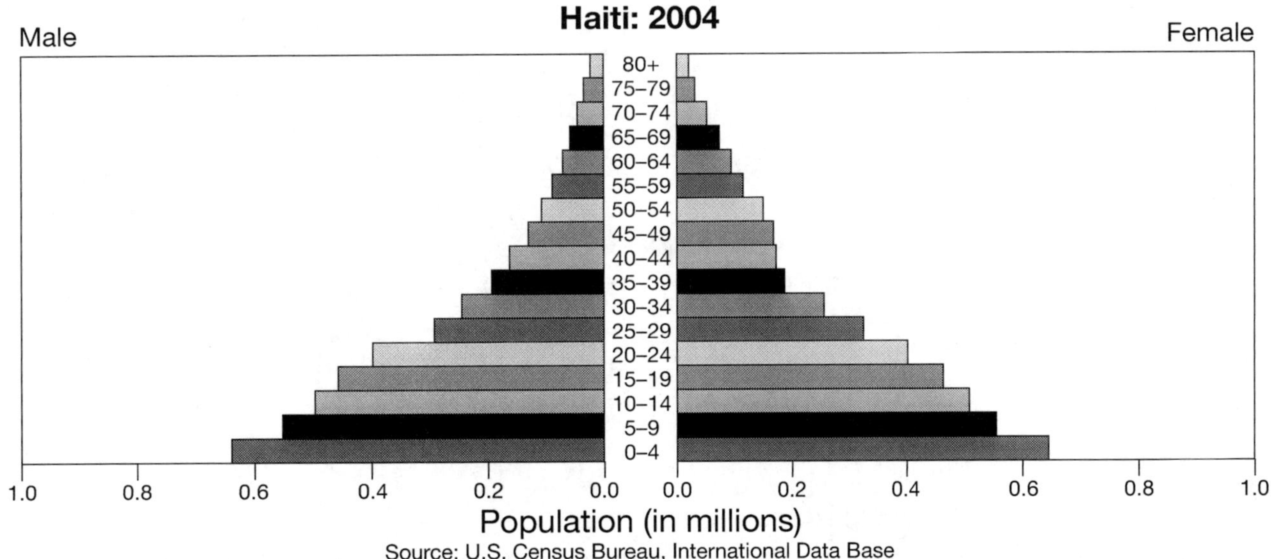

1. What age range makes up the largest group in Haiti? __________

2. Compare the number of males that are 0 to 19 years old with the number that are 65 and older.

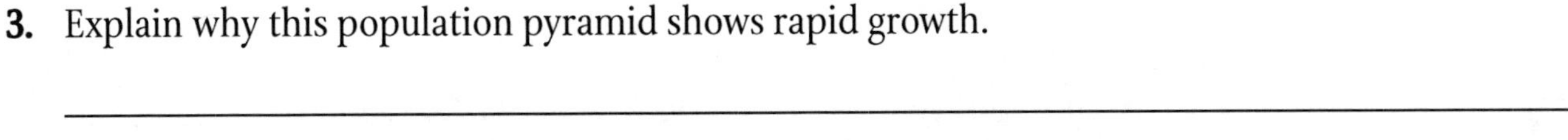

3. Explain why this population pyramid shows rapid growth.

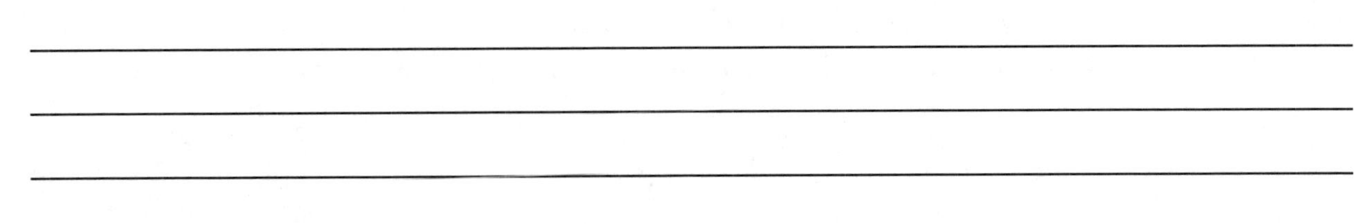

NAME:

UNIT 2 • ACTIVITY 20
Political Divisions in Latin America

Use the clues to complete the puzzle below. Look at a political map of Latin America for help.

Across

1. This country borders Mexico and Guatemala.
3. This sea contains the islands of Cuba, Jamaica, Puerto Rico, and the Bahamas.
6. This is a small coastal country south of Brazil.
7. This Central American country borders the United States.
8. This country shares an island with the Dominican Republic.
9. This is a Central American country connecting South America and North America where a famous canal is located.

Down

1. This is the largest country in South America.
2. The southernmost tip of South America is very close to the continent of ________________.
4. This is the larger of the two landlocked countries in South America.
5. This country is named for the line of latitude that runs through it.

NAME:

UNIT 2 • ACTIVITY 21
Water in Latin America

Read the chart. Then, on another sheet of paper, answer the questions that follow.

Statistics	Panama Canal	Suez Canal
Year built	Begun by French in 1880; finished by United States in 1914	Started by ancient Egyptians; modern canal begun in 1859 by French
Length of time to build	34 years	10 years
Obstacles to construction	Difficult geography and climate (tropical forests, mountains, heavy rains, strong currents), disease (malaria, yellow fever, tuberculosis, cholera, diphtheria, smallpox, bubonic plague), money, and technical know-how.	Money; diplomatic issues among French, British, and Egyptians; technical issues. Used forced labor.
Cost of construction	French and American $639,000,000; 80,000 people worked on it, 30,000 people died.	$114,000,000
Result of canal opening	Saved 7,872 miles on trip from NYC to San Francisco	Increased Europeans' access to Africa, allowing them to colonize more quickly. Saved 3,728 miles on the trip around Africa to the Indian Ocean.
Length of canal	50 miles	101 miles
Length of time to travel the canal	8–10 hours	16 hours south, 11 hours north
Maximum ship length	970 feet *	1,650 feet
Maximum ship beam	106 feet *	231 feet
Maximum ship draft	39.6 feet *	69.3 feet
Locks	3 locks	No locks. The canal is at sea level.
Connects which water bodies	Pacific Ocean to Atlantic Ocean	Mediterranean Sea to Red Sea (Indian Ocean)
In 2004, % of world trade that flowed through the canal	5% (13,000–14,000 ships passed through)	14% (15,000 ships passed through)

* This means that many of the modern supertankers are too big to use the Panama Canal.

1. Which canal was more expensive to build, took longer, and yet was shorter?
2. Compare the results of canal construction.
3. How do both canals continue to benefit world trade today?
4. The United States was able to finish building the Panama Canal because of medical advances. Speculate which new medicines allowed them to overcome the challenges of construction in Panama.

NAME:

UNIT 2 • ACTIVITY 22
The Amazon River

The Amazon is the second-longest river in the world at around 4,000 miles long. It is number one in terms of volume of water carried. The Amazon is responsible for about 20% of the total volume of freshwater entering the world's oceans. During the rainy season, the Amazon can be up to 25 miles wide! It drains about 40% of all of South America, including much of the area occupied by the world's largest tropical rain forest. It flows through Peru, Bolivia, Venezuela, Columbia, Ecuador, and Brazil. Cities along it include Iquitos and Manaus, both cities founded by the Portuguese, which became major rubber producers in the nineteenth century. Today, tourism and trade in Amazonian hardwoods and brazil nuts are profitable businesses. The river is so deep that ocean-going ships can navigate two thirds of the way up it. Since so much of the river flows through tropical rain forests, the human population along the river, outside of a few urban areas, is relatively low. About 200,000 people from about 170 Indian cultural groups live there. Local people have a wealth of knowledge of the river system and its vegetation and wildlife. These people are threatened as the rain forest faces challenges from mining, cattle ranchers, deforestation, and increasing development. Over 2.5 million acres of rain forest has disappeared in recent years.

You have been invited to participate in a "parade of rivers." Your task is to use what you have learned from the information above to create a sketch below of a parade float that highlights the Amazon River. Include on your float the physical type of geographic area that the river runs through. Your float might include signs with the names of large cities along the river, any threats the river basin area faces, a symbol you design, or a slogan you write that sums up your sketch.

NAME: ______________________________

UNIT 2 • ACTIVITY 23
Latin American Landforms

The Trans-Amazon Rally in May, 1986, began with over 100 teams anticipating an 8,700-mile journey. After the cars were shipped to Cartagena, Colombia, the organizers informed the drivers that there was not enough money to run the race. Drivers took over, and the race began with an altered route and a good deal of adventure. The race ran for 26 days across 8,000 miles. Whoever was not ready to go each morning was eliminated, so the number of racers quickly declined. The first day was spent up in the mountains on bad gravel roads, at altitudes reaching 11,000 feet. Some roads had 1,000-foot drop-offs. There was also a risk of landslides, military skirmishes, terrorist activities, tear gas, and student demonstrations.

The trip continued through Ecuador (over the equator). Ecuador is a lush, green country of hilly pastureland and parts of the Amazon rain forest. The group next drove through Peru. Many teams lost valuable time getting lost or stranded because of poor road guides and language barriers. In Peru, the course went through 3,000 miles of arid desert along the coast with winding roads up into the Andes. While in Lima, Peru, for repairs, the racers surfed on the chilly South Pacific waves. They stayed overnight in Arica—the driest place on Earth. There has been no measurable precipitation there for over 400 years.

In Chile, they passed copper mines, looking at the volcanoes of Bolivia in the distance. After crossing the deserts, fewer than 50 cars were left to cross into Argentina over the snow-draped mountains on the highest road in the world. Drivers described the autumn foliage and chilly air of Argentina (remember this is the Southern Hemisphere, so May is fall) as a welcome contrast to the Chilean deserts. They went over the pampas, passing cattle and farm towns along the way. Only 15 vehicles finished the race in Buenos Aires, Argentina.

Answer the following questions.

1. Which countries did the drivers drive through? ______________________________

____

2. What different types of geographic landscapes did they encounter on their journey?

____

____

3. If you were to decide to participate in this road race, name at least three things you would make sure you knew about this region in advance.

____

____

____

NAME:

UNIT 2 • ACTIVITY 24
Climate Comparison

On another sheet of paper, make a climograph for each city based on the charts below. Then answer the questions that follow.

Manaus, Brazil, is at about 3° 8' S 60° 0' W.
Average Temperature and Precipitation

	Jan	Feb	Mar	Apr	May	Jun	Jul	Aug	Sep	Oct	Nov	Dec	Year
°F	78.8	78.8	78.6	78.8	79.2	79.3	79.7	81.0	81.5	81.5	80.8	79.9	79.8
inches	10.4	10.3	11.7	11.1	8.0	4.1	2.6	1.8	2.5	4.4	6.3	8.7	81.9

São Paulo, Brazil, is at about 23° 30' S 46° 40' W.
Average Temperature and Precipitation

	Jan	Feb	Mar	Apr	May	Jun	Jul	Aug	Sep	Oct	Nov	Dec	Year
°F	70.2	70.5	69.4	66.0	61.9	59.7	58.6	60.6	62.4	64.4	66.4	68.7	64.9
inches	8.9	8.2	6.3	2.8	2.7	2.1	1.4	1.9	3.0	4.6	5.5	7.3	54.7

Quito, Ecuador, is at about 0° 13' S 78° 30' W.
Average Temperature and Precipitation

	Jan	Feb	Mar	Apr	May	Jun	Jul	Aug	Sep	Oct	Nov	Dec	Year
°F	56.5	56.1	56.5	56.3	56.8	56.1	56.5	56.7	56.7	55.8	55.6	56.1	56.3
inches	3.5	5.3	5.8	6.5	4.3	1.9	1.1	1.4	3.3	5.3	3.9	3.7	46.0

La Paz/Alto, Bolivi, is at about 16° 30' S 68° 9' W. Altitude: 12,000 feet above sea level.
Average Temperature and Precipitation

	Jan	Feb	Mar	Apr	May	Jun	Jul	Aug	Sep	Oct	Nov	Dec	Year
°F	49.8	49.5	49.6	48.9	47.3	45.1	44.4	46.2	48.2	50.4	51.6	50.7	48.6
inches	5.1	4.1	2.8	1.9	0.5	0.2	0.3	0.6	1.2	1.6	2.0	3.7	24.0

1. Which two cities have the most even temperature all year long? What do these cities have in common? (*Hint:* Look at their latitude.) ____________________

2. In which city does elevation affect temperature the most? ____________________

3. Manaus is located in the Amazon rain forest. Precipitation does fall all year, but there is still a wet season and a slightly drier season. When is the "dry season"? ____________________

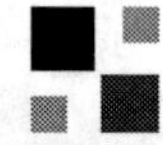

NAME:

UNIT 2 • ACTIVITY 25
Food in the Americas

Many everyday foods originated in the Americas before the arrival of Columbus in the fifteenth century. The people in the Americas had long grown corn as well as beans, squash, avocado, tomatoes, sweet potatoes, vanilla beans, and chili peppers. In the Andes, farmers grew beans, peanuts, and potatoes as well. Incan farmers had even learned how to freeze-dry the over 100 varieties of potatoes they grew. Today, much of what is sold at grocery stores comes from Latin America. Goods such as bananas, sugar, cacao (chocolate), coffee, wheat, and beef are just a few of the agricultural products that are imported.

Write a menu and grocery list below for what you need to make three typical meals for your family. Use at least ten of the products mentioned above in your list. Underline those items on the list below. Do not worry about every ingredient. Just think about the main ones.

Menu: Meal One	Grocery List
____________________	____________________
____________________	____________________
____________________	____________________
____________________	____________________
____________________	____________________

Menu: Meal Two	Grocery List
____________________	____________________
____________________	____________________
____________________	____________________
____________________	____________________
____________________	____________________

Menu: Meal Three	Grocery List
____________________	____________________
____________________	____________________
____________________	____________________
____________________	____________________
____________________	____________________

On another sheet of paper, write a short paragraph supporting or arguing against the following statement: I live in a global grocery store.

NAME:

UNIT 2 • ACTIVITY 26
Urban Centers in Latin America

Answer the questions, using information from the following reading and the chart.

Over the past two decades, many Latin Americans have moved to cities. This process is called *urbanization*. People have made the decision to move for many reasons. They include the hope for a better job, a desire to move away from parents, a lack of land to farm in rural areas, or a conflict in the countryside. Cities have also been growing rapidly as populations increase. The movement of these new people into the cities has made it important for governments to continue to improve services in the cities. This is hard in developing countries. Issues of housing, safe drinking water, sanitation, education, and security are all costly but important.

Four of the 20 largest urban areas in the world are in Latin America.

Rank (in 2004)	Urban Area	Population
3	Mexico City	21,500,000
5	São Paulo	19,100,000
17	Buenos Aires	13,250,000
20	Rio de Janeiro	11,600,000

1. What is urbanization? ______________________________

____

2. Why have people moved to cities? ______________________________

____

____

3. What effect do you think this has had on public services in the cities?______________________________

____

____

4. On another sheet of paper, make a recommendation to the mayor of any one of these four cities regarding what you think he or she should do about services.

NAME:

UNIT 3 • ACTIVITY 27
Population Density

Look at the chart below. Then answer the questions that follow.

Rank	Country	Area in sq km	Population est. 2004	Humans/ sq km
1	Bangladesh	144,000	141,340,476	982
2	Taiwan	35,980	22,749,838	632
3	Occupied Palestinian Territory	6,220	3,636,195	585
4	South Korea	98,480	48,598,175	493
5	Puerto Rico	9,104	3,897,960	428
6	Netherlands	41,526	16,318,199	393
7	Lebanon	10,400	3,777,218	363
8	Belgium	30,510	10,348,276	339
9	Japan	377,835	127,333,002	337
10	India	3,287,590	1,065,070,607	324
11	El Salvador	21,040	6,587,541	313
12	Sri Lanka	65,610	19,905,165	303
13	Rwanda	26,338	7,954,013	302
14	Israel	20,770	6,199,008	298
15	Philippines	300,000	86,241,697	287
16	Haiti	27,750	7,656,166	276
17	Vietnam	329,560	82,689,518	251
18	Jamaica	10,991	2,713,130	247
19	United Kingdom	244,820	60,270,708	246
20	Germany	357,021	82,424,609	231

1. What are the four European countries listed in the chart? __________

2. Which of the European nations is the most densely populated? __________

3. What country on the list has the largest territory, yet also the largest population? Compare the population density of that country with number 1 on the list. __________

4. The population of the United States is 293,027,751 people. The area of the United States (the third largest country in the world) is 9,629,091 square kilometers. What is the population density of the United States? __________

   How does this compare to the other 20 countries on the list? __________

NAME:

UNIT 3 • ACTIVITY 28
Population Distribution in Hungary

Look at the population pyramid for Hungary below. Then answer the following questions. Pay close attention to the population number in thousands.

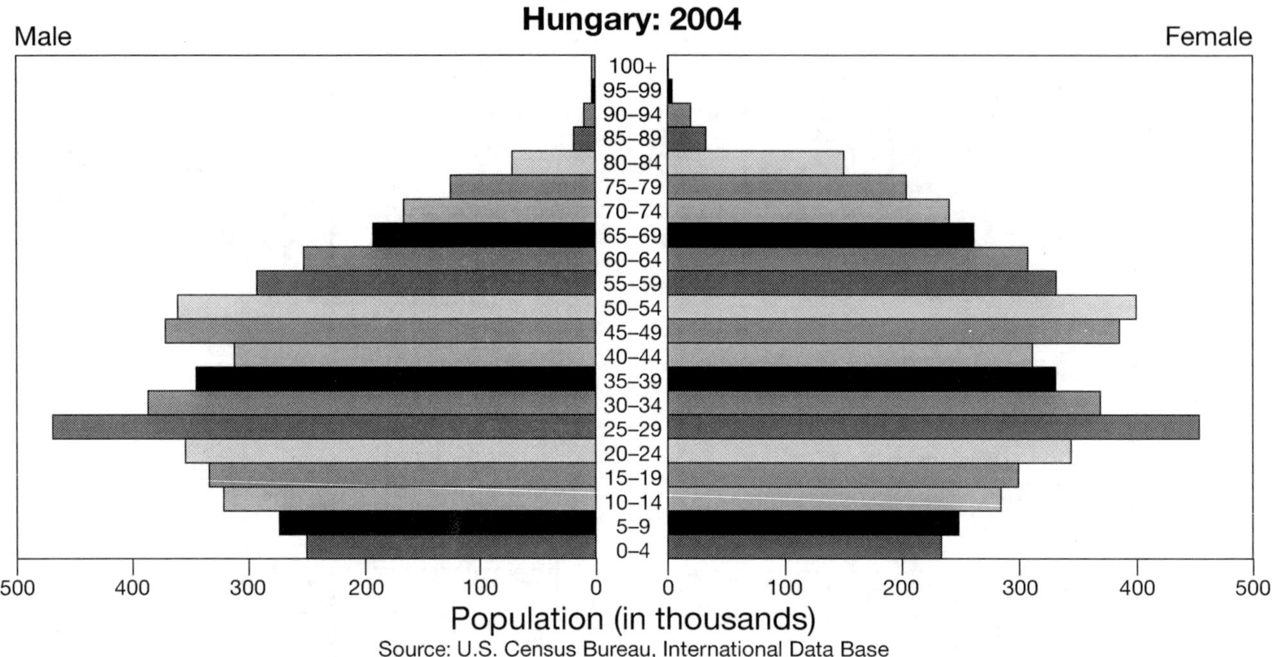

1. What age range is the largest group in Hungary? ______________________

2. Roughly add up the population of Hungary that is under 25. Add up the population 60 and over. Combine these two numbers. Add up the population between the ages of 25 and 59. (This is the part of the population most likely to be working.) Which number is greater? What does this mean? ______________________

____

____

3. Explain why this population pyramid shows negative growth. ______________________

____

____

NAME:

UNIT 3 • ACTIVITY 29
Political Divisions in Europe

Use the clues to complete the crossword puzzle.

Across

5. This country has experienced continuously changing borders in the twentieth century due to changing political rule.
7. France, Italy, and Spain all have a border on this sea.

Down

1. The alpine nations are all very ________________.
2. This peninsula includes Greece and the nations of the former Yugoslavia.
3. This country borders France, Germany, Luxembourg, and the Netherlands.
4. This is called the breadbasket of the east due to high grain production.
6. Scandinavia includes Denmark, Iceland, Sweden, Finland, and ________________.
8. The British Isles include Ireland, Northern Ireland, Scotland, Wales, and ________________.

NAME:

UNIT 3 • ACTIVITY 30
Landforms of Europe

On the map, label the significant peninsulas, islands, and bodies of water listed below. Then answer the questions that follow. You may consult an atlas, if necessary.

Scandinavian peninsula	Corsica	Black Sea
Denmark (Jutland peninsula)	Crete	Bosporus Strait
Iberian peninsula	Baltic Sea	Strait of Gibraltar
Italian peninsula	North Sea	English Channel
Balkan peninsula	Mediterranean Sea	
Sicily	Adriatic Sea	

Looking at your completed map, answer the following questions.

1. Which peninsulas would have benefited most from the calm waters of the Mediterranean Sea?

____

2. Which warm water strait would Russians have been likely to try to gain access to in order to trade in the Mediterranean Sea? _______________

____

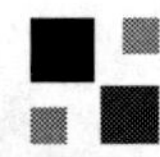

NAME:

UNIT 3 • ACTIVITY 31
The Danube

The Blue Danube, Johann Strauss's most famous waltz, was written in nineteenth-century Austria. The harmony of the song captured the spirit of Vienna. As the second-longest river in Europe, the Danube flows from the Black Forest in Germany 1,770 miles to the east. It ends in Romania as it empties into the Black Sea. The river is used for trade, fishing, irrigation, and hydroelectric power.

As one of Europe's major waterways, it has transported soldiers for nearly 2,000 years beginning with the Romans. Access to and use of the river has been the subject of many treaties among European powers. No one wanted one country to control its mouth, since so much commercial traffic also traveled along it. More recently, nations have attempted to divert part of the river for hydroelectric power, causing further disputes.

Important cities on the Danube include Vienna, Budapest, Bratislava, and Belgrade. The Danube flows through eleven countries in Europe. Through canals, it is connected to three other major river systems as well as the North and Black seas. As a result, the river remains critical for European trade. Over 3,500 vessels pass yearly through its delta. Due to human overuse, there are many current environmental concerns. These include a decrease in local wildlife, especially fish and birds; raw city sewage; chemicals from industrial waste and mining discharge; and agricultural run-off.

Using reference material or the Internet, research one of the cities mentioned above. Then, create a poster advertising the city to possible tourists. Use photographs, drawings, and other graphics. Choose a type that is big and easy to read. Make sure you include something that shows how the city is connected to the Danube. Create your poster on poster board for display in the classroom. Write the name of the city below, and use the rest of this page for notes.

City on the Danube ______________________________

Notes: ______________________________

____

____

____

____

____

____

____

____

____

____

____

NAME:

UNIT 3 • ACTIVITY 32
The Winter Olympics

Imagine that you are on the International Olympic Committee. You are trying to decide if the Winter Olympics should be held again in the Alps region of Europe. Read the information below. Then answer the questions that follow.

The European Alps extend over 600 miles through France, Switzerland, Germany, Liechtenstein, Italy, Slovenia, and Austria. During the warmer months, many tourists and locals enjoy hiking along mountain trails as well as through the numerous nature parks. In the wintertime, ski resorts count on snowfall to bring in skiers from across the globe. The Alps attract 100 million tourists annually. The Alps have been the site of numerous Winter Olympics. However, some people worry that global warming has decreased snowfall in Europe in recent years.

Olympics in the Alps

1924	site of first winter Olympics, Chamonix, France
1928	St. Moritz, Switzerland
1936	Germany's Bavarian Alps (Garmisch and Partenkirchen)
1948	St. Moritz, Switzerland
1956	Cortina d'Ampezzo, Italy (snow trucked in by Italian soldiers)
1964	Innsbruck, Austria (snow again trucked in)
1968	Grenoble (French alps)
1976	Innsbruck, Austria (snow again trucked in)
1992	Three Valleys region, Albertville, France
2006	Sestriere region, Italian Alps

1. How many times have the Winter Olympics been held in Europe? ____________________

2. How many different countries in the Alps region have hosted the Winter Olympics? ________

3. Name at least two potential problems you see with having the Olympics in the Alps.

____

____

4. Imagine you are a member of the International Olympic Committee. On another sheet of paper, write a short essay either supporting or not supporting a decision to host the Olympics in the Alps.

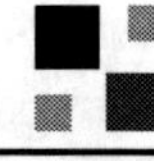

NAME:

UNIT 3 • ACTIVITY 33
Climate in Europe

On another sheet of paper, create three climographs using the information shown in the chart below. Then answer the questions that follow.

Helsinki-Vantaa, Finland, is at about 60° 10' N 25° 0' E.
Average Temperature and Precipitation

	Jan	Feb	Mar	Apr	May	Jun	Jul	Aug	Sep	Oct	Nov	Dec	Year
°F	21.0	20.3	25.7	35.6	47.3	57.2	62.2	59.9	51.3	41.9	32.7	25.7	40.1
inches	1.8	1.4	1.4	1.5	1.7	1.8	2.4	2.9	2.6	2.7	2.6	2.2	25.0

London/Heathrow, U.K., is at about 51° 30' N 0° 10' W.
Average Temperature and Precipitation

	Jan	Feb	Mar	Apr	May	Jun	Jul	Aug	Sep	Oct	Nov	Dec	Year
°F	40.8	40.3	44.8	48.2	54.7	60.1	65.1	64.0	59.4	53.6	45.9	43.0	51.7
inches	2.4	1.4	2.0	1.7	1.8	1.8	1.8	1.7	1.7	2.9	1.8	2.3	23.3

Istanbul/Ataturk, Turkey, is at about 41° 0' N 28° 58' E.
Average Temperature and Precipitation

	Jan	Feb	Mar	Apr	May	Jun	Jul	Aug	Sep	Oct	Nov	Dec	Year
°F	42.1	42.3	44.6	52.5	60.8	69.3	73.9	74.1	68.0	60.1	52.9	46.8	57.3
inches	3.7	2.8	2.3	1.7	1.2	0.9	0.7	0.6	1.1	2.1	3.5	4.0	24.6

1. Which city has the coldest winter (the most months below freezing)? ____________________

2. Which months are the summer months for these three cities? ____________________

____

3. Compare the precipitation in each of these locations. Which city has a slightly drier summer than the others? ____________________

NAME:

UNIT 3 • ACTIVITY 34
Tulip History

Look at this time line of significant events in tulip history. Then answer the questions below. (*Note:* Holland and the Netherlands are the same country. People who live there are called the Dutch.)

1000 C.E.	Records show that tulips were in cultivation in Turkey. Tulips originally came from farther west in Central Asia, Armenia, and Persia.
12th century	Omar Khayyam, Iranian poet, mathematician, and astronomer, writes a love poem mentioning tulips.
13th century	The Sufi poet Rumi sings the praises of tulips in many songs in the Persian empire (present day Iran/Afghanistan).
1520–1566	The Tulip Era takes place in Turkey under Suleiman II.
1593	Carolus Clusius plants the first tulip in the Botanical Gardens in Leiden, Netherlands. This is the beginning of hybrid tulips in Europe.
1610–1637	Tulipmania in Holland. Growth in the tulip trade causes tulips to become overvalued. The tulip market crashes in 1637, leaving thousands bankrupt.
17th–18th century	Tulips are included in the paintings of famous artists, such as Breughel and other Dutch masters.
1700–1730	Tulipmania in Turkey. Mohammed Lalizari is a tulip fan. He imports thousands of bulbs to Turkey from the Netherlands.
1730	Sultan Ahmed III (the ruler of the Ottoman Turks) is brought to trial for crimes including "having spent too much money on the traditional annual tulip festivals." He is beheaded.
1960	In the Netherlands, a celebration takes place of the 400-year existence of tulips in western Europe.
2004	There are more than 3,500 tulip hybrids grown in the Netherlands; over three billion tulip bulbs are produced each year. Two billion of these are exported, mostly to the United States. The value of this trade is close to $2 billion.

1. From where did tulips spread to Europe? ________________________________

2. What are three examples of how the love of tulips was reflected in art and literature? ________

____

3. How did tulips bankrupt many people in the Netherlands? ________________________

____

4. Which country is the largest importer of Dutch tulips? ________________________

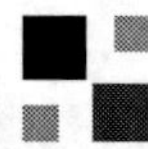

NAME:

UNIT 3 • ACTIVITY 35
Industry Comparisons

Look at the pie chart below, and then answer the questions. (*Note:* The countries where coal production was under 1% of the global total were added together. In this pie chart, the top five producers are included, as well as all European coal producers.)

Global Coal Production, 2003

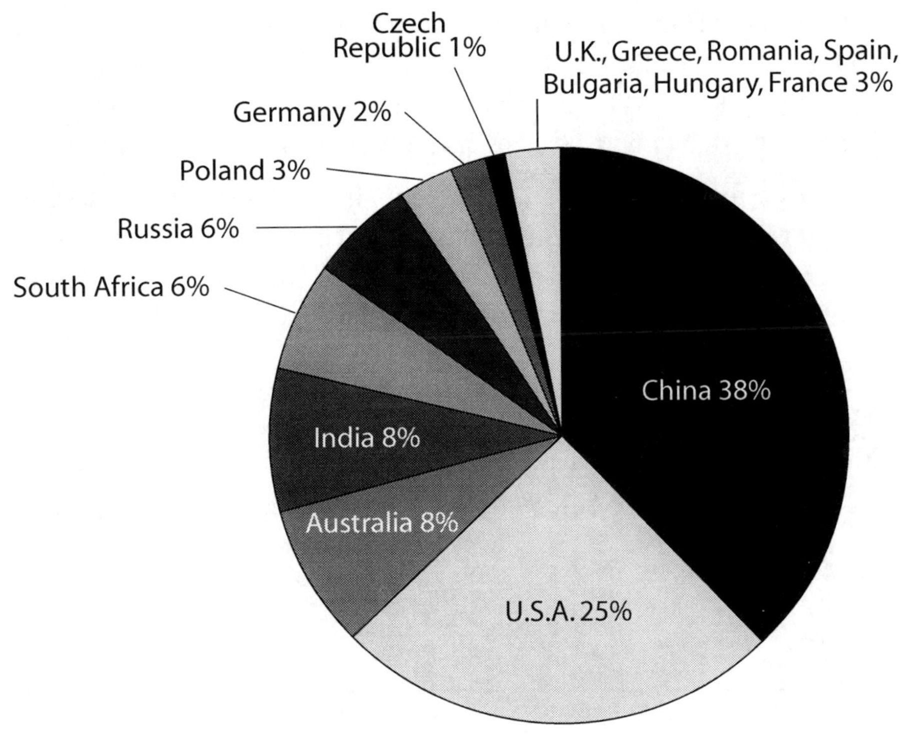

1. Which country is the largest producer of coal in the world? ______________________

2. The top four producers of coal total what percentage of global coal production? ____________

   ____

3. European coal producers total approximately what percentage of the global pie? (Include Russia in this calculation.) ______________________

4. According to the reading in your text, how important is coal as an energy source in Europe?

   ____

NAME:

UNIT 3 • ACTIVITY 36
The Berlin Wall

When World War II ended in 1945, the city of Berlin was divided into four parts: British, American, French, and Soviet. The Soviet section in the east included the city of Berlin. By 1948, the Berlin Blockade began, prohibiting goods from the west from coming into the city by road or rail. In 1948, the United States began the Berlin Airlift, sending needed supplies into the city by air.

In 1949, Germany was officially divided into two separate countries: the German Democratic Republic (East Germany) and the Federal Republic of Germany (West Germany). In 1961, the Berlin Wall was built, and no travel between East and West Berlin was allowed. The wall was 96 miles long, made of barbed wire and concrete. West Berliners were allowed to travel to the east by 1963, but East Berliners could not go to the west. Many tried to escape and were shot trying to go over the wall.

On November 9, 1989, as reforms were happening throughout eastern Europe and in the Soviet Union, the Berlin Wall was opened. Pieces of the wall were saved as historic artifacts and can be found all over the world, representing the power of freedom. On October 3, 1990, Germany was reunited. The former path of the Berlin Wall is now marked by a row of paved stones.

Imagine that it is November 1989. You have lived in West Berlin since World War II. Write a letter to your cousin in East Berlin describing how you feel about being able to finally visit her.

November 1989

Dear ____________________,

____

____

____

____

____

____

____

____

____

____

____

____

NAME:

UNIT 4 • ACTIVITY 37
Location: North Africa

North Africa refers to the northernmost region of Africa bordering the Mediterranean Sea. These five countries—Morocco, Algeria, Tunisia, Libya, and Egypt—are north of the Sahara Desert. North Africans historically have been connected to people in southern Europe and the Middle East through culture and trade.

On the map, label the places listed below. Then answer the questions that follow.

Bodies of water: Strait of Gibraltar, Mediterranean Sea, Nile River, Suez Canal

Countries: Morocco, Algeria, Tunisia, Libya, Egypt

Capital cities: Rabat, Algiers, Tunis, Tripoli, Cairo

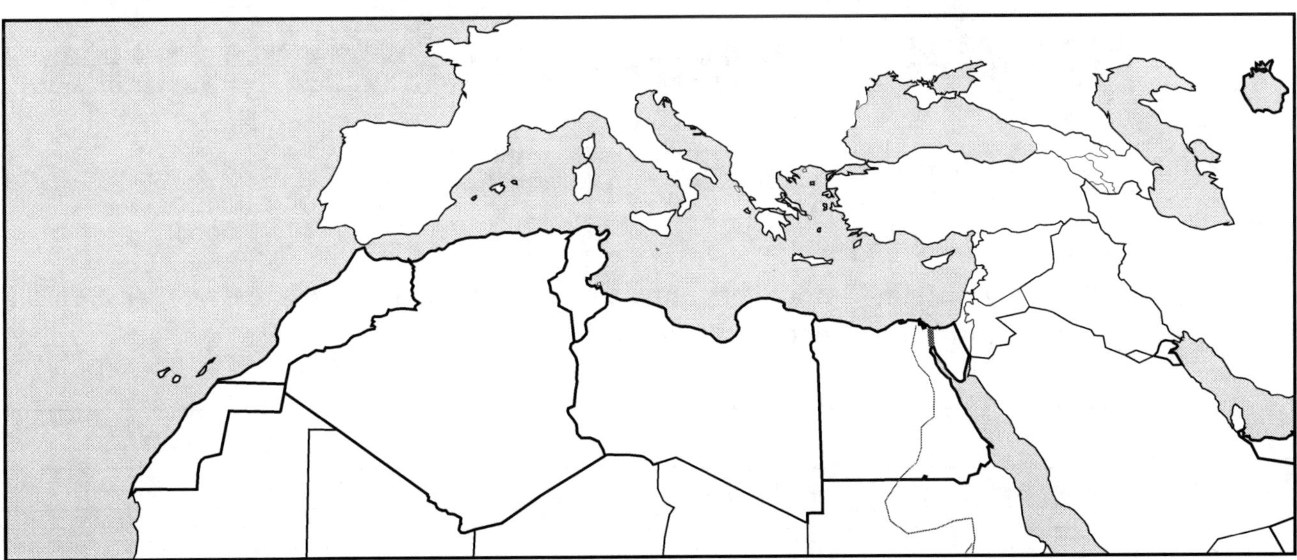

1. Why are four of these capital cities located on the coast? ____________________

   ____

2. What body of water has historically connected southern Europe, the Middle East, and North Africa? ____________________

3. Choose one of the countries of North Africa. Research that country and write a brief report on the country. Include its history, people, climate, and economy. Use a separate sheet of paper for your report.

NAME:

UNIT 4 • ACTIVITY 38
Population in Morocco

Look at the population pyramid for Morocco. Then answer the following questions. Pay close attention to the population number in millions.

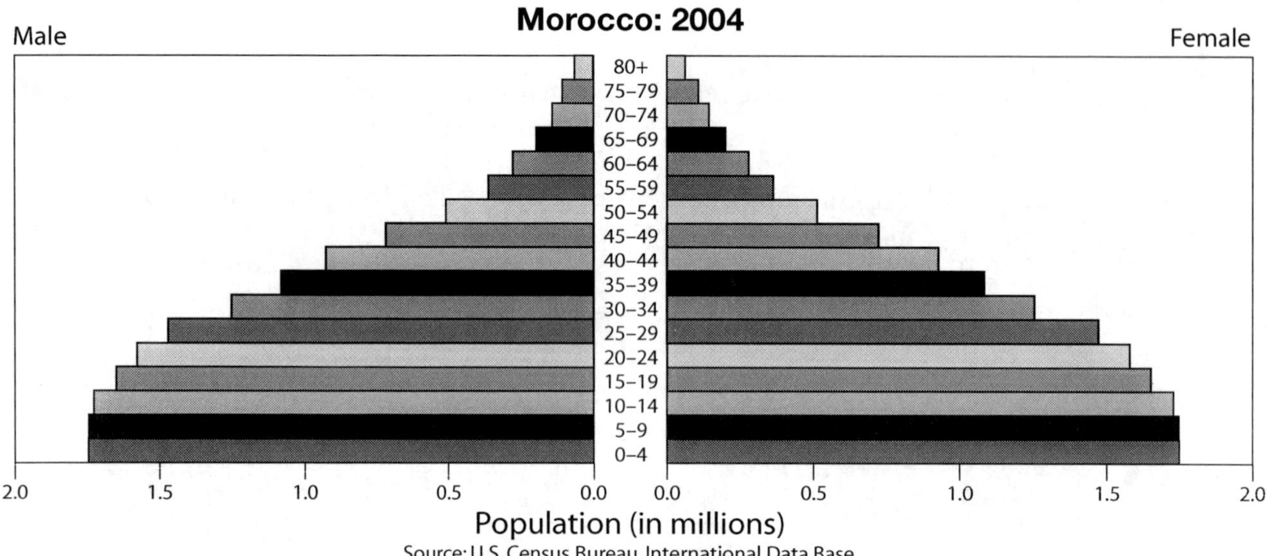

1. "Population growth in Morocco has remained at approximately the same rate for the last 20 years." Why is this a true statement? Explain.

____

____

____

____

2. What percentage of the population is under the age of 20 in this pyramid? ______________

3. Why does this population pyramid shows rapid growth overall? Explain. ______________

____

____

____

____

NAME:

UNIT 4 • ACTIVITY 39
Water in North Africa

Use the clues to complete the crossword puzzle.

1 2 3 4 5 6 7

Across

5. All North African countries border this body of water.
6. This is the world's longest river.
7. There are few peninsulas, inlets, or ________ on the North African coast.

Down

1. The Suez Canal was built as a quicker way to the ________ Ocean.
2. North African ships can also eventually reach the Pacific Ocean by rounding the ________ of Good Hope.
3. North African ships must go through the Strait of ________ to reach the Atlantic Ocean from the Mediterranean Sea.
4. These are areas fed by underground water reserves in the desert.
5. The Strait of Gibraltar has the tiny Gibraltar colony owned by Spain to its north and the country of ________ to its south.

NAME:

UNIT 4 • ACTIVITY 40
The Nile

The world's longest river is the Nile. It starts in Burundi and flows northward through northeastern Africa before draining into the Mediterranean Sea. It is 4,132 miles long. The Nile River Basin includes parts of Tanzania, Burundi, Rwanda, the Democratic Republic of the Congo, Kenya, Uganda, Ethiopia, Sudan, and Egypt. Over 60 million Egyptians depend on the Nile for their freshwater supply. The Nile gets its name from the Greek word *Neilos,* which means "valley" or "river valley." The flooding along its banks has historically left fertile black silt that helped this area support early societies and farming. The people who lived along its banks thousands of years ago used irrigation. They were also the first to use the plow. Since the river flooded at regular times, its people did not experience unexpected, damaging, and deadly flooding.

Parts of the Nile are navigable, allowing transportation and trade along it. The Aswan Dam was completed in 1970 and has been a source for hydroelectric power, irrigation, and crop protection. The building of the dam did destroy some ancient Egyptian archeological sites, and the dam now prevents the regular flooding of the river. This means that this relatively poor country must purchase fertilizer that was once provided by flooding. Environmental concerns include water quality and availability because of the large population that lives along the Nile.

Your task is to use what you have learned from the information above and from other resources to create a travel brochure. Your brochure should highlight the Nile River in a way that will make people want to visit it. Do some research using reference books and web sites. Download pictures or make some drawings that show attractive features of the Nile and the areas it flows through. Include important sights along the Nile (there are many to choose from!). Write the information for your brochure in clear, descriptive language. Use the space below to take notes or to design your brochure.

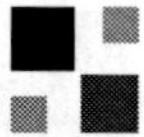

NAME:

UNIT 4 • ACTIVITY 41
A Mystery Place in North Africa

Read the following clues, and try to guess the mystery place! Then draw what you imagine it looks like.

1. This place has a name that repeats itself (in two different languages).
2. About 10,000 years ago, this place had vast underwater reserves, so people were able to herd cattle here. Giraffes were able to eat branches off trees. Cave art and satellite photos showing dried-up riverbeds are all that remain.
3. Heavy rainstorms can drown everyone suddenly if they seek refuge in wadis.
4. "Ships" can travel for days through this landform.
5. There are lush, green areas scattered throughout this area.
6. Nighttime and winter temperatures can get quite chilly.
7. Most of this area is covered by rock, gravel, and stones.
8. This landform rarely enjoys rainfall.

Mystery place: ______________________

How it looks:

NAME: ___

UNIT 4 • ACTIVITY 42
Climate of Fez

Plot data from the chart on the climograph below. Then answer the questions that follow.

Fez, Morocco, is at about 34° 05' N 5° 0' W.
Average Temperature and Precipitation

	Jan	Feb	Mar	Apr	May	Jun	Jul	Aug	Sep	Oct	Nov	Dec	Year
°F	48.6	51.6	55.8	58.6	65.7	72.9	79.0	79.3	73.9	64.9	57.0	50.2	63.1
inches	3.0	2.5	3.0	2.5	1.3	0.5	0.0	0.1	0.5	1.7	3.0	3.3	21.4

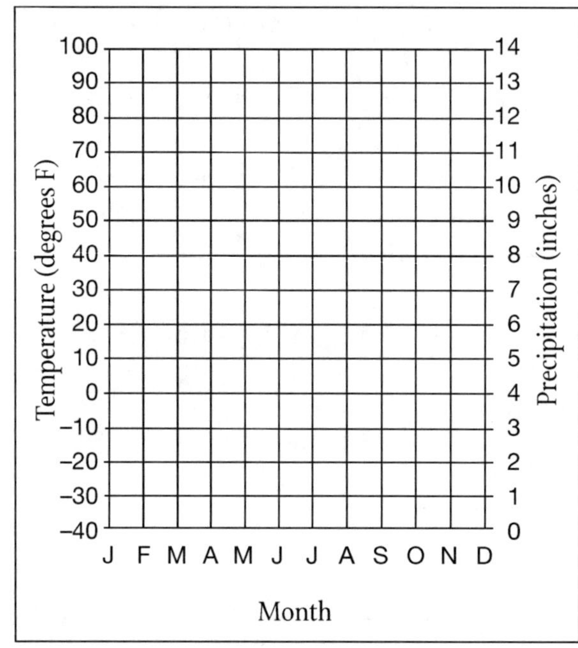

1. What is the difference in degrees between the coldest and warmest months? ___

2. Is there a “wet” season and a “dry” season? Why or why not? ___

3. Would you expect to find a seasonal change of clothing? What kinds of different clothing might be needed? ___

4. Looking at the climograph, how can you tell Fez is located in the Northern Hemisphere? ___

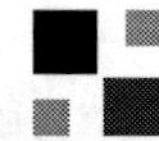

NAME:

UNIT 4 • ACTIVITY 43
Farming in Dry Lands

Read the passage below. Then complete the three-frame diagram that shows how the region has changed over time. Draw a picture in each frame that shows the region in the time period.

North Africa is notable for its lack of arable land for farming. As a result, wheat, a hardy plant that can grow in unfavorable conditions, is a staple throughout the region. In addition, peanuts, barley, and dates are grown. In the more temperate climates along the Mediterranean, Morocco and Algeria produce fruit, including grapes for wine, and olives. In Egypt, irrigation has for thousands of years provided good farming along the Nile River. Livestock also grazes on these lands. But the increasing desertification does not support much grazing. Ten thousand years ago on the Tasili Plateau (on the edge of the Sahara in Morocco), cave paintings were drawn that showed savanna (grassland). It had vegetation, such as trees high enough for giraffes. The paintings also show domesticated cattle in great numbers by a river. Even 1,000 years ago, these routes were busy with trade caravans traveling from Mecca and Cairo to the great West African empires. Today, satellite photos show the dried riverbed under the desert.

Change Over Time: Agriculture in North Africa

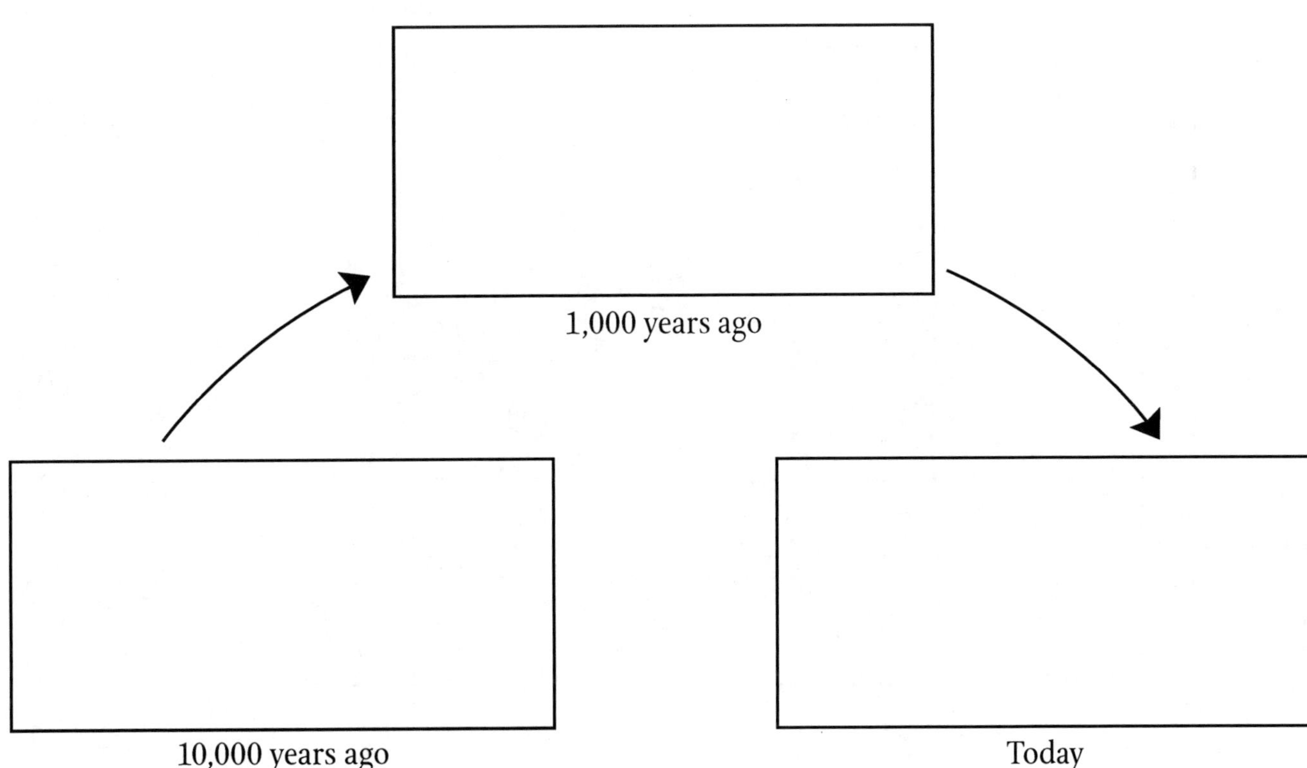

NAME:

UNIT 4 • ACTIVITY 44
Resources: North Africa

Create a resource map for North Africa, using the outline map below.

Labels

1. Label Morocco and Western Sahara, Algeria, Tunisia, Libya, and Egypt.
2. Label the Mediterranean Sea and the Nile River.
3. Label the Sahara Desert.

Symbols

For each of the following resources, create a different symbol for your key. Then add the symbol(s) on the map in the correct locations.

1. oil
2. natural gas
3. iron
4. phosphates—used in fertilizer

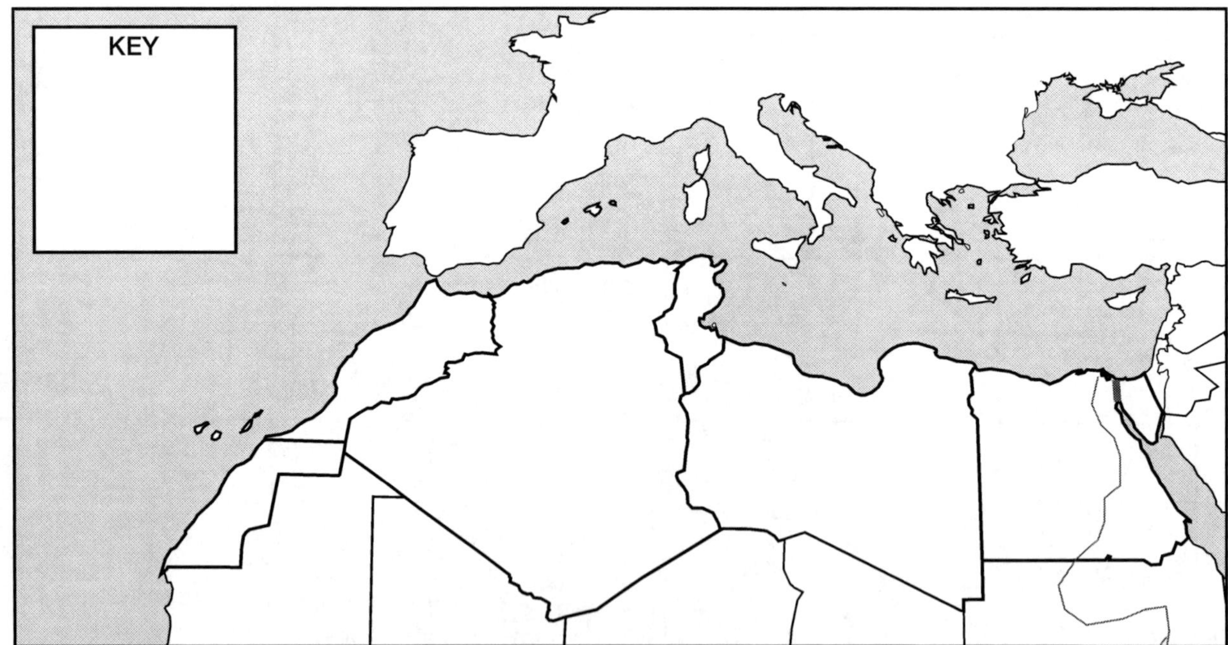

NAME:

UNIT 4 • ACTIVITY 45
Location: Sub-Saharan Africa

Use the clues to complete the crossword puzzle.

Across

3. The four countries on the Horn of Africa in desert fringe are Somalia, ____________, Eritrea, and Djibouti.
4. ________________ is the largest island nation of Africa.
7. ________________ in southern Africa is surrounded by Angola, Namibia, South Africa, Zimbabwe, and Zambia.

Down

1. This is a west African nation that was formed by freed African-American slaves in the nineteenth century.
2. To its east, this country borders the Indian Ocean, to the north Lake Victoria, and to the west, Lake Tanganyika.
3. Much of sub-Saharan Africa lies below the Sahara Desert and below the __________________.
5. A country in Central Africa that has changed its name several times in recent years is the Democratic Republic of the ________________.
6. The Prime Meridian passes through two desert fringe, landlocked countries: Burkina Faso and ____________.

NAME:

UNIT 4 • ACTIVITY 46
Comparative Urbanization

Urbanization can be defined as the process by which cities grow and become more densely populated. Countries have become increasingly urbanized as people move to the cities for jobs, as farmland disappears, and as population increases. When there is rapid urbanization, sometimes problems occur. Governments cannot keep up with the demand for services, such as housing, water, sewage, education, and transportation. In addition, there are often environmental effects and widespread unemployment.

The bar graph below shows the percentage of the population that is urbanized (lives in cities). Use the graph to answer the questions that follow.

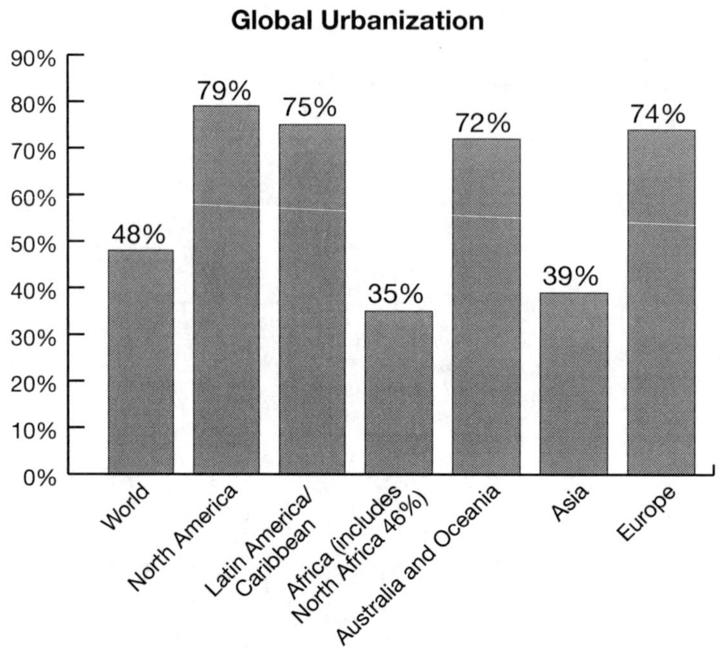

1. Which region has the highest percentage of people living in cities? ______________________

2. Which region has the lowest percentage of urbanization? ______________________

3. Each percentage represents an average within the region. This means that there are some countries within the region that have a higher percentage of people living in cities and some that have a lower one. Based on this chart, what conclusions about urbanization would you make? For example, would you be able to say that Canada is as urbanized as the United States? Why or why not?

____

____

____

NAME: ____________________

UNIT 4 • ACTIVITY 47
Urbanization in Africa

Look at the bar graph showing urbanization in some African nations. Use it to answer the questions that follow.

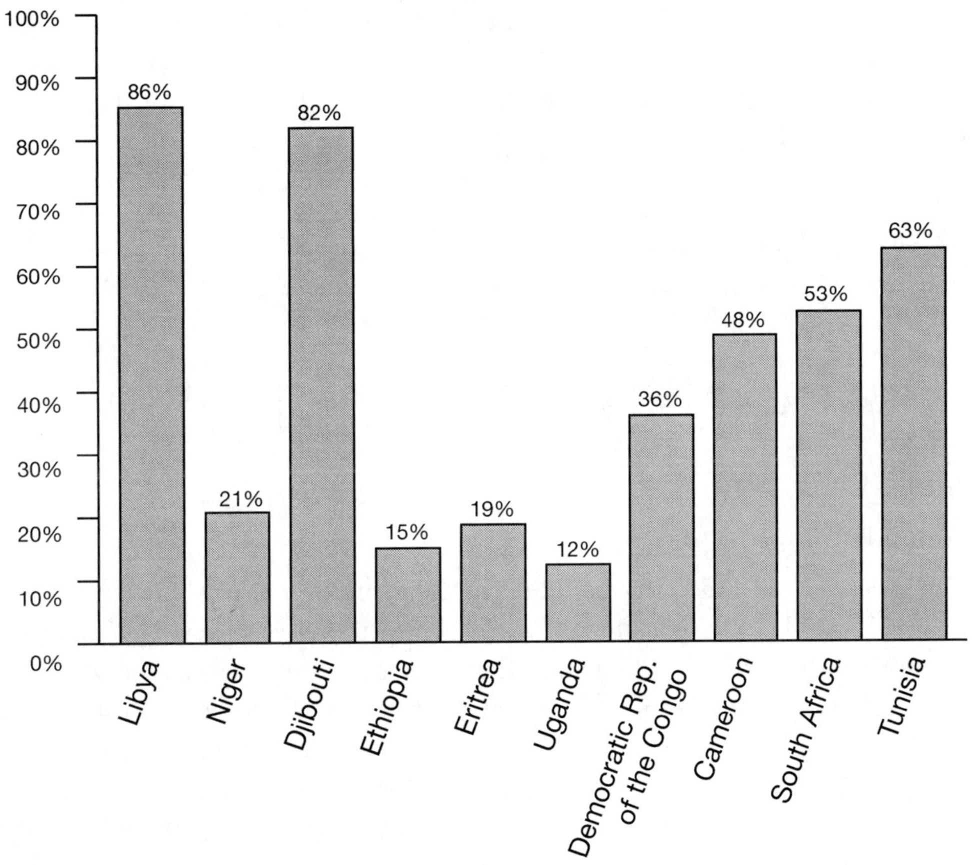

1. Eighty-six percent of Libyans live in urban areas. Why? (Think about the geography of the rest of the country.)

____

____

____

2. Which African country has the lowest urban percentage of population? ____________

3. Djibouti, Eritrea, and Ethiopia are all located in the same geographic area. Why do you think their urban percentage rates are so different? ____________________

____

____

____

NAME:

UNIT 4 • ACTIVITY 48
Around the Capes

In 1998, Karen Thorndike became the first American woman to sail solo around the world. In a 36-foot yacht named after Amelia Earhart, she sailed 33,000 miles over a two-year period. She sailed around (rounded) the world's five great capes: Cape Horn (tip of South America), Cape of Good Hope (South Africa), Cape Leeuwin (south of Perth, Australia), South East Cape (Tasmania), and Southwest Cape off New Zealand. Students all over the world wrote her e-mails asking questions about sailing, science, and more.

Read Thorndike's descriptions below. Then, on a separate sheet of paper, write her a letter, asking questions about her voyage. Try to include at least five questions in your letter.

"No one knows how big and powerful the ocean can be until you look at it from the deck of a small boat. I am in awe of the size and strength of the waves."

Rounding Cape Horn

"The waves and swells that build up in the proximity of the Horn are vicious and the effect of being behind land was astonishing. That enormous relentless swell was gone. Three hours after rounding, the fog lifted from the coast and I saw Cape Horn. The source of my focus and worries for the last 2 months. Even at 12 miles away it looked as inhospitable as one could imagine. It has been calculated that before the Panama Canal and the Trans-American Railway the number of vessels that sailed these waters was immense. Somewhere in the neighborhood of 20,000 per year with a count of 40 ships that could be sighted on a clear day off the Horn. Unless disaster struck crews could expect to round the Horn possibly 30 times in their careers. In a very serious and old tradition the Cape Horn mariners would get an earring after rounding the Horn. It was a sign to other sailors that they had been around the most feared and the greatest cape of all. I do not have pierced ears but for this accomplishment I will join that club of tradition."

Cape of Good Hope and Agulhas

"The morning should see me past Cape of Good Hope and past Cape Agulhas by nighttime. Lying 30 miles south and 60 miles east of Good Hope, Cape Agulhas is really the most southerly tip of Africa. Known for having bad weather and monster seas, it is also called "The Cape of Storms."

NAME:

UNIT 4 • ACTIVITY 49
Lake Victoria

Lake Victoria is Africa's largest lake and the world's second-largest freshwater lake. It is bordered by three countries: Uganda, Kenya, and Tanzania. The following are recent actions that have placed the lake ecosystem in danger.

- Nile perch was introduced to Lake Victoria in the 1950s by the British for sport-fishing. It fed on the smaller fish. Since the perch was an oily fish, people preserved it by smoking. This led to lakeside deforestation.
- Of the original 500 native lake species, 300 are now thought to be extinct.
- Increased population growth in the area has led to more farming and fishing.
- Raw sewage and chemical pollution has caused algae and weeds to grow out of control.
- Weeds cause difficulties in moving boats and ferries across the lake and disrupt use for fishing, hydroelectric power, and drinking water.
- The Lake Victoria basin supports one of the densest and poorest rural populations in the world (up to 1,200 persons per square kilometer).

Using the information above, imagine what the point of view would be of each of the following people. Write a sentence in each speech bubble that captures that person's opinion about the condition of Lake Victoria.

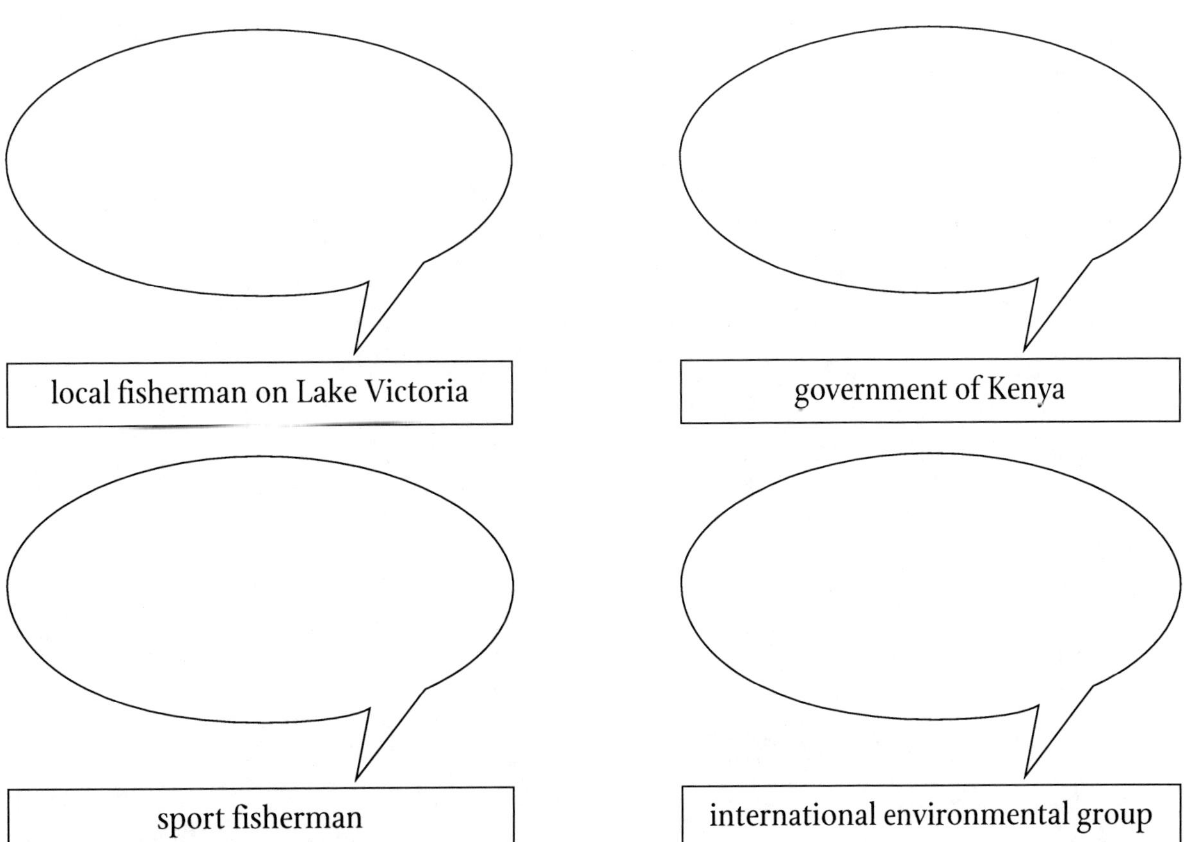

NAME:

UNIT 4 • ACTIVITY 50
The Congo River

Many rivers flow into the Congo River, a fact that gave the river its name: "Congo" means the "river that swallows all rivers." The Congo is Africa's most important transportation system. It is the second-longest river in Africa (second to the Nile). It flows through the Democratic Republic of the Congo, the People's Republic of the Congo, Zambia, Tanzania, Angola, Cameroon, and the Central African Republic. The Congo River system drains an area the size of Europe. It takes six months for water to travel from the source to the Atlantic Ocean. Much of the river is not navigable, due to cataracts and waterfalls, as well as islands, in the very wide parts of the river and also at its mouth. Much of the river flows slowly while winding through tropical forests. But the last 220 miles are a series of 32 falls, cataracts, and gorges known as the Livingstone Falls. The river's basin is bordered by areas of savannah (grasslands). Despite the fact that river traffic cannot go all the way to the Atlantic Ocean, barges do go up and down sections of the river, carrying fuel, wood, minerals, and agricultural produce. Important cities include Cabinda at the mouth, Kinshasa, Brazzaville, and Kisangani.

You have been invited to participate in a "parade of rivers." Your task is to use what you have learned from the information above to create a sketch below of a parade float that highlights the Congo River. Included on your float should be the physical type of geographic area that the river runs through. Your float might include signs with the names of large cities along the river, any threats the river basin area faces, a symbol you design, or a slogan you write that sums up your sketch.

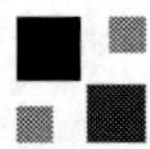

NAME:

UNIT 4 • ACTIVITY 51
Landforms of Sub-Saharan Africa

Use words from the box to fill in the missing parts of the story. Then write your own ending to the story.

Congo River	Great Rift Valley	Namib Desert	Sahel
deforestation	Kalahari Desert	plateaus	
glaciers	Mount Kilimanjaro	Sahara Desert	

Rebecca and Jesse were traveling to Africa for the first time. As they flew over the continent, they expected to see green jungle everywhere. Instead, they saw desert, grasslands, and some rain forest along the **1.** ________________ basin in Central Africa. They were surprised when they flew over Egypt and saw the Nile River flowing north through the desert with a narrow strip of green on either side. As they flew south of Egypt, they could see the **2.** ________________, which they had read was expanding due to desertification. As they got off the plane in Ouagadougou, the capital of Burkina Faso, they were in the **3.** ________________, semiarid desert fringe lands. From there, they voyaged south to Central Africa where they saw the effects of **4.** ________________. Local forests were cleared, and erosion had washed away good soil. They continued, and reached the dry **5.** ________________, stretching along the southwestern coast of Africa. Going east from there, they found themselves on a high, flat piece of land, one of many **6.** ________________ that make up much of Africa. In Botswana, the dry **7.** ________________ spread across south Central Africa, making their journey difficult. They continued north and went on a safari in the Okavango delta, where they saw many interesting animals. As they went northeast by train, they crossed through the huge fault zones of the **8.** ________________. Here they could see where the land had separated hundreds of thousands of years ago, making it ideal for archeologists to search for fossils. In some cases, the land has been filled in by lakes. As they reached the eastern coast of Africa, they saw Mount Kenya and **9.** ________________, originally volcanoes. **10.** ________________ are still found on top today, making beautiful views of snowcapped mountains on the equator.

____

____

NAME:

UNIT 4 • ACTIVITY 52
Climatic Differences

On another sheet of paper, create a climograph for each of the following cities. Then answer the questions that follow.

Cape Town, South Africa, is at about 33° 55' S 18° 22' E.
Average Temperature and Precipitation

	Jan	Feb	Mar	Apr	May	Jun	Jul	Aug	Sep	Oct	Nov	Dec	Year
°F	69.8	70.0	67.8	63.1	58.8	55.6	54.3	55.4	57.7	61.2	64.8	67.8	62.2
inches	0.6	0.6	0.9	1.9	3.6	4.1	3.6	3.3	2.1	1.6	1.0	0.8	24.1

Kinshasa/N'Djili, Democratic Republic of the Congo, is at about 4° 15' S 15° 22' E.
Average Temperature and Precipitation

	Jan	Feb	Mar	Apr	May	Jun	Jul	Aug	Sep	Oct	Nov	Dec	Year
°F	77.4	77.7	77.5	77.7	76.6	73.2	70.9	73.2	76.1	77.2	76.8	77.0	75.9
inches	5.4	5.8	7.2	8.6	5.7	0.2	0.1	0.1	1.6	5.2	9.3	6.1	55.3

Nairobi/Kenyatta, Kenya, is at about 1° 25' S 36° 50' E.
Average Temperature and Precipitation

	Jan	Feb	Mar	Apr	May	Jun	Jul	Aug	Sep	Oct	Nov	Dec	Year
°F	67.1	68.4	69.1	68.5	66.6	63.9	62.2	63.0	65.5	67.5	66.7	66.7	66.3
inches	1.8	1.7	2.9	6.3	4.7	1.2	0.5	0.5	1.0	1.7	4.7	3.0	30.0

Tombouctou (Timbuktu), Mali, is at about 16° 50' S 3° 1' E.
Average Temperature and Precipitation

	Jan	Feb	Mar	Apr	May	Jun	Jul	Aug	Sep	Oct	Nov	Dec	Year
°F	68.4	73.0	79.2	86.4	91.2	91.9	89.8	85.5	86.4	84.9	76.1	69.1	81.8
inches	0.0	0.0	0.0	0.0	0.1	0.7	2.4	3.1	1.3	0.1	0.0	0.0	7.7

1. Which city has a definite wet and dry season? ______________________

2. Which city is most likely located in the Sahel? ______________________

3. Which city most likely has a tropical rain forest nearby? ______________________

4. Which city is not in the Southern Hemisphere? ______________________

5. Which cities are nearest the equator? ______________________

NAME:

UNIT 4 • ACTIVITY 53
Diamonds

Read the tour description of Kimberly, South Africa, below.

Kimberley, South Africa

Diamonds were found mainly in India for over 1,000 years. After their discovery in Brazil and Venezuela, the world turned its attention there. It was not until 1867 that the first diamond was found in South Africa, by a farm boy. In 1888, Cecil Rhodes founded the De Beers mining company.

The Kimberley Mine Museum is an authentic re-creation of the 1880 diamond rush. You can visit the places diggers lived, stores, pubs, the Boxing Academy, and the farmhouse of the De Beers family. During the height of the diamond rush, 30,000 miners dug here, living in shanty towns made of tin. There was little water and no sanitation.

The diamond displays in the museum include the famous Eureka diamond, the first registered diamond in South Africa. It is a 616-carat rock! Most impressive is the Big Hole. It is 215 meters (705 feet) deep and has a diameter of 1.6 kilometers (1 mile), making it the largest human-dug hole in the world. Diggers removed 2,772 kilos of diamonds from this hole with just picks and shovels.

The mines themselves go down 1,097 meters. During the Boer War in 1899, when the city of Kimberley was under siege, women and children hid inside the mines to escape the shelling. Although the Kimberley mines ended operation in August 1914, the site remains an important place to remember the rich history of mining in South Africa. The De Beers Company also runs a tour of the Bultfontein Diamond Mine. It is the only underground tour of a diamond mine in the world. Here will you learn about the dangerous conditions men worked under as they sweated and often died deep beneath the surface of the earth in the hopes of making it rich on diamonds.

Today, South Africa remains an important diamond producer. However, Australia has become the top exporter of diamonds. Botswana is the world's second-largest producer, and Russia is the third-largest producer.

On another sheet of paper, write a song from the point of view of a diamond miner. Be sure to include information from the paragraphs above about living and working conditions in the mines.

NAME: ______________________________

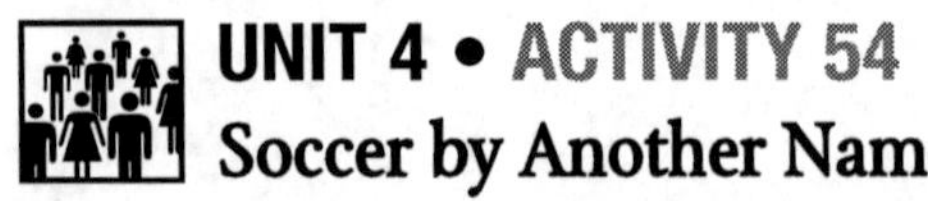

UNIT 4 • ACTIVITY 54
Soccer by Another Name

The game of "football" became popular in Britain in 1846. But it was not the same game that Americans know. In other countries, "football" refers to the game that Americans know as soccer.

As the British Empire grew in the late 1800s, soldiers, traders, engineers, and sailors from Britain traveled around the world. They brought football with them. The first match in South Africa occurred in 1862. At first, the game was a symbol of colonial control. People under British rule began to adopt British culture, such as football, in replacement of traditional activities. But eventually the game became a way to resist British rule. As local people began to play the game well, they gained some hope that they could beat the British at more than just a game. Today, football is played by more than 240 million people in more than 200 countries. The World Cup, soccer's world championship tournament, will be held in Africa in 2010.

Imagine that you live in Capetown, South Africa, in 1899. The British have recently defeated the Dutch settlers in your country. But this means little to you, since you do not have a say in the colonial government anyway. Europeans will continue to make all the laws. It doesn't matter if they are British or Dutch. You have a job carrying bags for the British army. During breaks, the soldiers play football. They are looking for teams to play against. So many of the local people are learning how to play.

In the space below, write a dialogue between a British soldier and you as a Capetown resident learning to play football. You can ask about rules, about history, about Britain, and so on.

You: ______________________________

Soldier: ______________________________

You: ______________________________

Soldier: ______________________________

You: ______________________________

Soldier: ______________________________

You: ______________________________

Soldier: ______________________________

You: ______________________________

Soldier: ______________________________

You: ______________________________

Soldier: ______________________________

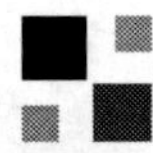

NAME:

UNIT 5 • ACTIVITY 55
Location and Time Zones

Russia is so large that it spans eleven time zones. This means that when it is 1:00 P.M. in St. Petersburg in the west, it is midnight on the Kamchatky peninsula in the far east of the country. The map below shows the approximate locations of the time zones.

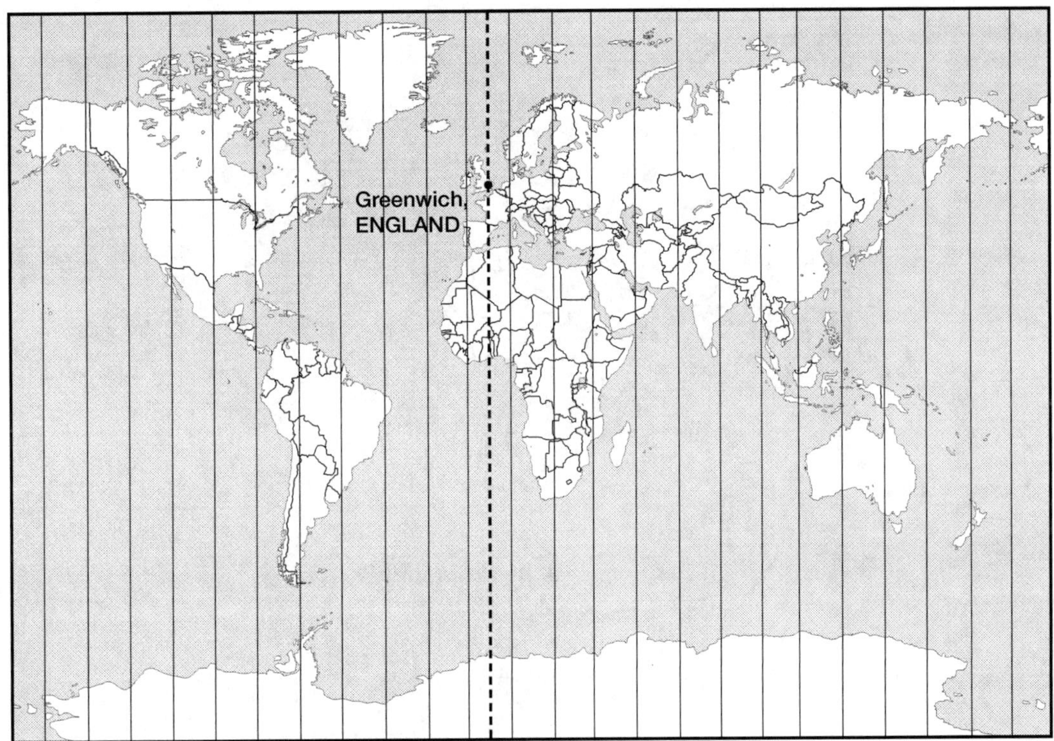

Imagine that it is noon in Greenwich, England. What time would it be if you went to the following places? (Remember, you are adding or subtracting the number from noon, depending on if you are going east or west.) Use the map above.

1. Moscow, Russia ________________
2. Beijing, China ________________
3. Cape Town, South Africa ________________
4. Buenos Aires, Argentina ________________
5. Mexico City, Mexico ________________
6. Vancouver, British Columbia, Canada ________________
7. New York City, U.S. ________________
8. Anchorage, Alaska, U.S. ________________

NAME:

UNIT 5 • ACTIVITY 56
Population: Russia and Uzbekistan

Look at the population pyramids for Russia and Uzbekistan below. Then answer the following questions on another sheet of paper. Pay close attention to the population number in millions.

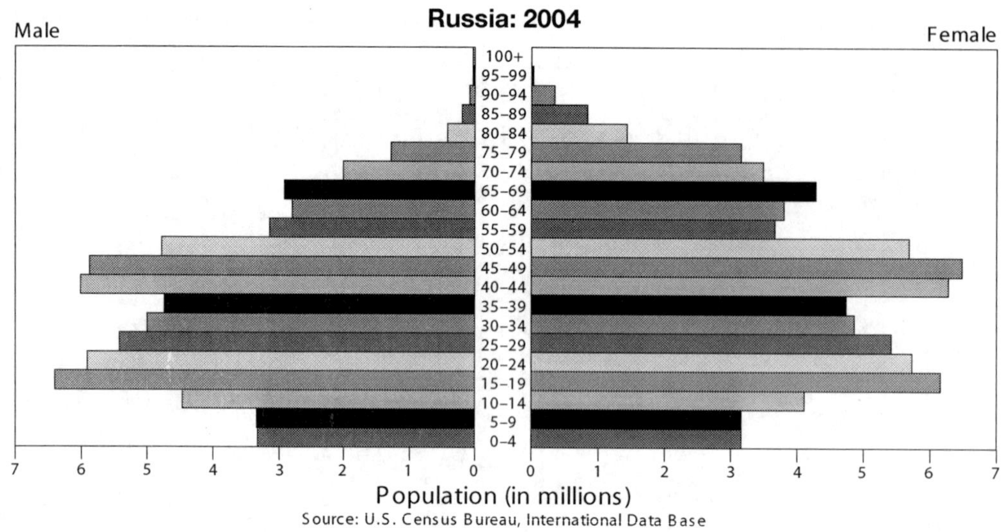

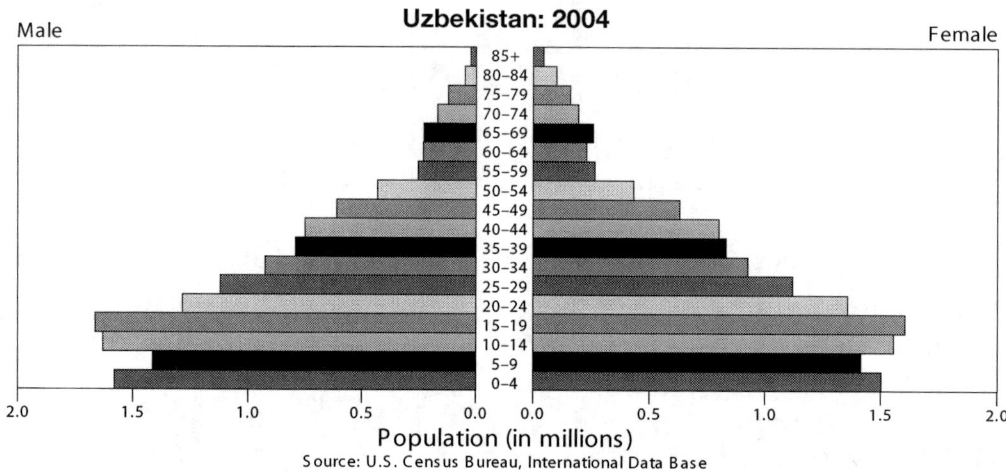

1. What is the total approximate population of Russia?
2. Russia is the largest country in the world (it is almost twice as large as the next largest country). Yet it is seventh in population. What might explain this low population if Russia has all that space?
3. What age range makes up the largest group in Russia?
4. What age range makes up the largest group in Uzbekistan?
5. Compare the two pyramids in terms of gender, numbers, and patterns. Identify if they represent rapid, slow, or negative growth (or some combination). Guess why there might be more females in Russia between the ages of 65 and 95 than in Uzbekistan.

NAME:

UNIT 5 • ACTIVITY 57
The Trans-Siberian Railway

By the mid-1800s, Russia had expanded its territory through Siberia as far as the Pacific Coast. In 1860, Russians founded the city of Vladivostok on the coast. It became a useful trading post and port. The Russians had always wanted a port on the Pacific for trading and military purposes. But transportation across Siberia was difficult. The Russians needed a way to get from their cities in the west of the country to their new port in the east. They built the Trans-Siberian Railway.

The Trans-Siberian Railway was begun in 1891, after years of debate. Many foreign engineers criticized the plan for the railway because so much of it was made of wood. The railway is more than 10,000 kilometers (6,000 miles) long. It was the first overland link between western Europe and the Far East.

Building started from both ends of the railway and worked inward. Convict labor and soldiers did most of the work. Many cities in Siberia began as railway towns, since laborers needed a place to settle temporarily. The work was slow. Many workers were far from home. Supplies were scarce, and the climate and terrain were harsh. The work on the railway was delayed by conflicts.

The line was partially funded by France. And an agreement with China was needed because the railway cut through a portion of Chinese territory. The eastern section was particularly difficult to build because of Lake Baikal and the mountains beyond it. The lake was crossed in sleighs until this part of the line was complete.

In 1904, Japan invaded Russia before the railroad was completed. During the early stages of the war, problems with the railway surfaced. The single-track railway was not suited to moving the heavy guns and other equipment from western Russia to the east. By 1905, however, rail improvements had made the situation better, but not enough to defeat Japan in the war.

By 1916, the railroad along the Chinese border was complete. The Trans-Siberian is still the world's longest railway line. You can travel the length of it today—in about seven days!

Using a map of Russia from an atlas or an on-line resource, locate the following cities. The Trans-Siberian Railway still runs through them. Then research one of the cities. Write a short description of the city on another sheet of paper. Explain why you think the railway was routed through that city.

Moscow	Vladivostok
Omsk	Ekaterinburg
Belogorsk	Khabarovsk
Ulan Ude	Irkutsk
Krasnoyarsk	Yaroslavl

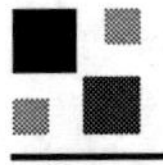

NAME:

UNIT 5 • ACTIVITY 58
Western Russia and Central Asia

Use the clues to complete the puzzle.

Across

2. This peninsula is on the Pacific seaboard of Russia.
3. The Barents, Kara, and Laptev seas flow north into the ___________ Ocean.
5. For most of the year, much of Russia's coastline is icebound, and there is no access to the sea. During that time, the country is ___________.
7. This term describes seas that are entirely surrounded by land.

Down

1. This sea divides Russia from its Central Asia neighbors.
3. This sea in Central Asia is shrinking because of heavy water use for farming.
4. A body of water that forms a natural boundary between Russia and its Eastern European neighbors is the ___________. (2 words)
6. These islands on the eastern Russian coast stretch toward Japan.

NAME:

UNIT 5 • ACTIVITY 59
The Volga

The Volga is the longest river in Europe. Referred to as Mother Volga, it is considered the lifeblood of Russia. Over 40% of Russians (over 60 million people) live near it and its tributaries, including half of all Russian farmers. Irrigation, hydroelectricity, fishing, and trade are the main uses of the river. There are eight major hydroelectric stations along the river. They generate power for much of Russia. Since the river is navigable for most of its over 2,300-mile length, trade has been an important part of its history. It was used for Viking trade through eastern Europe over 1,000 years ago. More recently, it was used to move soldiers during World War II. There are now more than 900 ports and 550 industrial docks along the Volga's banks. Current environmental threats include industrial waste and agricultural runoff. These affect the quality of the water and the fish stocks.

Using reference material or the Internet, research the Volga River and some cities it flows through. Some of those cities are:

- Moscow
- Saratov
- Nizhniy Novgorod
- Volgograd
- Kazan
- Astrakhan
- Samara

Choose one city, and create a poster advertising the city to possible tourists. Use photographs, drawings, and other graphics. Choose type that is big and easy to read. Make sure you include something that shows how the city is connected to the Volga. Create your poster on poster board for display in the classroom. Write the name of the city below.

City on the Volga: ______________________________

NAME:

UNIT 5 • ACTIVITY 60
Landforms of Russia and Central Asia

As you read this travel diary entry, underline each landform that is mentioned.

Dear Diary,

Today I begin my adventure through Russia on the Trans-Siberian Railway! First, I travel through a great expanse of the North European Plain. I pass north of the Caucasus, where glaciers glisten on the tops of the mountains. I look out the train window and see the Ural Mountains looming before me!

I have now passed beyond the Urals and am on the West Siberian Plain. It reminds me of the grassy prairies found in the United States and Canada, alongside their transcontinental railways. As I continue east, I reach higher ground. Now I am on the Central Siberian Plateau. By the time I reach eastern Siberia, it will be quite mountainous.

I pass north of the Central Asian nations, but I meet new friends on the train who tell me all about them. Kazakhstan is mostly plains, where cattle are raised and cotton is grown. The Kara-Kum desert lies south of these plains through Uzbekistan and Turkmenistan. It is a vast expanse of black sand. Kyrgyzstan and Tajikistan are very mountainous and include the Tian Shan mountain range, which forms a border between these countries and China. *Tian Shan* means "Heavenly Mountains." The highest mountain peak in this region is Imeni Ismail Sumani Peak. It used to be known as Communism Peak.

My Central Asian friends have all disembarked by the time the train reaches Krasnoyarsk. This is a resting spot. . . . Travel to Irkutsk and the famed Lake Baikal is coming up. The lake is frozen as the train goes around it. Before the train line was finished, they used ferries to take the train and the people across. Next, I pass into the Manchurian part of the line. I will follow the Amur River, once a rich source of sable pelts during the height of Siberian fur trading. And then I will come to Vladivostok on the Sea of Japan, an ice-free harbor for at least part of the year.

Traveling the whole way through this immense country makes me truly appreciate the vast distances and differences in cultures that had to be spanned by a central government.

Sincerely,

A fellow traveler

NAME:

UNIT 5 • ACTIVITY 61
Climate in Moscow and Vladivostok

Create two climographs by plotting the precipitation and temperature from the charts below. Then answer the questions that follow, using another sheet of paper.

Moscow, Russia, is at about 55° 45' N 37° 35' E.
Average Temperature and Precipitation

	Jan	Feb	Mar	Apr	May	Jun	Jul	Aug	Sep	Oct	Nov	Dec	Year
°F	13.5	15.6	24.6	39.9	54.0	61.3	65.3	62.1	51.6	39.6	28.4	18.5	39.5
inches	1.4	1.1	1.3	1.5	2.0	2.6	3.2	2.8	2.3	2.0	1.7	1.7	23.6

Vladivostok, Russia, is at about 43° 10' N 132° 0' E.
Average Temperature and Precipitation

	Jan	Feb	Mar	Apr	May	Jun	Jul	Aug	Sep	Oct	Nov	Dec	Year
°F	7.3	13.3	26.8	39.6	48.9	55.9	64.2	68.4	61.0	48.0	30.4	14.2	39.8
inches	0.4	0.5	0.9	1.7	2.6	3.6	4.2	5.8	4.8	2.2	1.2	0.6	28.5

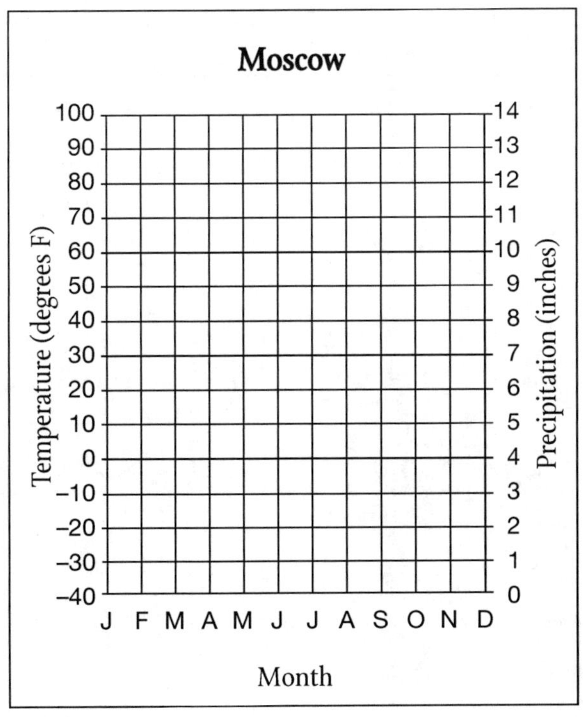

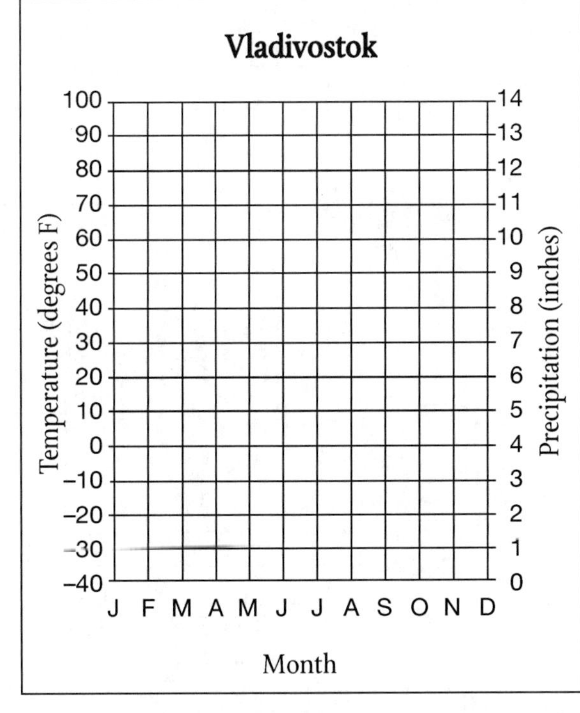

1. These two cities are at opposite ends of Russia. Compare their average year-round temperature and average year-round precipitation.
2. Compare the latitude of these two cities.
3. Draw conclusions about why you think the two cities have such similar climate records.

NAME:

UNIT 5 • ACTIVITY 62
The Fertile Triangle: Ukraine

Although much of Russia (90%) is not suitable for farming, the part that is suitable contains some of the richest soils in the world. Two thirds of Russia and Central Asia's agriculture occurs within this "fertile triangle." Wheat is the major product, but farmers also grow sunflowers, sugar beets, corn, cotton, and grapes.

Using colored pencils, color the map of Russia to show the fertile triangle. Follow these steps!

1. Label the Black Sea.
2. Label Russia, Belarus, Moldova, Ukraine, Georgia, and Kazakhstan.
3. Label St. Petersburg in the north.
4. Label Odessa in the west.
5. Label Novosibirsk in the east.
6. Draw lines to connect the three cities, forming a triangle.
7. Using a green pencil, shade in this region.
8. Create a key on your map indicating that this shaded area is the fertile triangle of Russia.

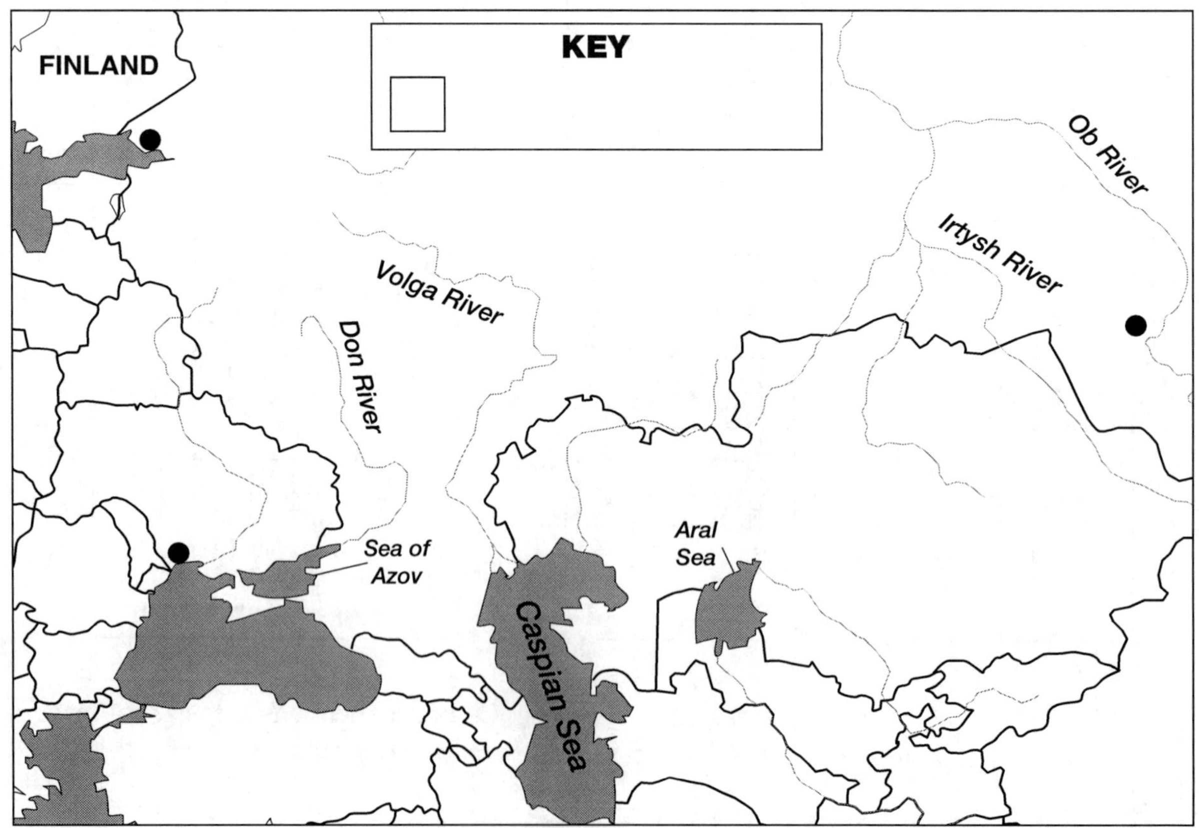

NAME:

UNIT 5 • ACTIVITY 63
Natural Resources Game

Imagine that you are a member of the Russian police forces hot on the trail of a resource thief. Follow the trail of clues, filling out the information along the way. Use an atlas to find the information.

1. Her first hit was at the Donets Basin (directly north of the Azov Sea). She got away from you there, making off with petroleum, natural gas, and coal. Record the latitude and longitude, and move on to another place in Russia that has petroleum and natural gas. ________________

2. You are now in southwestern Siberia. The train got stuck in the snow, so you have arrived in Omsk but have missed her again. She got away with more petroleum and gas. Record the latitude and longitude, and move on to a place known for its timber. ________________

3. You are now near Krasnoyarsk. The area around here is taiga, a wonderful place for timber production. You just cannot catch up to her! She is off again, this time with fresh timber. Record the latitude and longitude, and move on to a place known for its resident sable population. (Sables are small animals prized for their fur.) ________________

4. The Amur River is in eastern Siberia. You are so close that you can still see the footprints she made in the snow as she was releasing animals from their traps. But she flew out early this morning, back to the Ural Mountains. She is in search of hard minerals now. Record the latitude and longitude, and try to catch up. ________________

5. She is in the Urals now, near Magnitogorsk. You were very close, but she fled just before you arrived. She got away with iron ore, lead, copper, and zinc. Your only hint is that she has gone to seaside lowlands to gather salt and eat some caviar. Record the latitude and longitude, and get going. This is your last chance! ________________

6. Good thing you remembered the Caspian Sea's famous caviar. You were able to beat her here to the Caspian Depression and catch her red-handed as she was going for the salt and caviar found here. Record the latitude and longitude of the place of arrest. ________________

   Make a list below of all the resources you found in her possession.

   ____

   ____

   ____

   ____

   ____

NAME:

UNIT 5 • ACTIVITY 64
Local Government

In order to govern effectively, countries often have local governments to help make policy, carry out policies, and make government work better for its citizens. People like to have direct contact with their government representatives, and local government makes that possible. Usually, there are strict guidelines on what a local government can or cannot do. For example, in the United States, states cannot decide to go to war. But they can make educational policy for their citizens.

These local governments all have different names in different places. In Canada, South Africa, and China, for example, they are called provinces. In the United States and Australia, they are called states. They are emirates in the United Arab Emirates. And in Russia, they are called republics.

Imagine that you live in the eastern part of Russia. Write a letter to your local government officials thanking them for their work and asking them for help on some issue. Include references to the earlier activities you have done on time zones, climate, railroads, and population density.

NAME:

UNIT 5 • ACTIVITY 65
Location: The Middle East

The term *Middle East* refers to a region that shares historical, political, and cultural features. *Relative location* means a place's location in relation to other places. For example, the Middle East is west of South Asia, southeast of much of Europe, and northeast of much of Africa.

On the world map below, label the Middle East and the places listed. Color only the region of the Middle East when you have finished.

Water Bodies

Mediterranean Sea
Red Sea
Indian Ocean
Arabian Sea
Black Sea
Caspian Sea
Nile River
Persian Gulf
Indian Ocean
Suez Canal
Tigris-Euphrates River

Countries

Egypt
Bahrain
Iraq
Israel
Jordan
Kuwait
Lebanon
Oman
Qatar
Yemen
Cyprus
Iran
Turkey
Saudi Arabia
Syria
United Arab Emirates

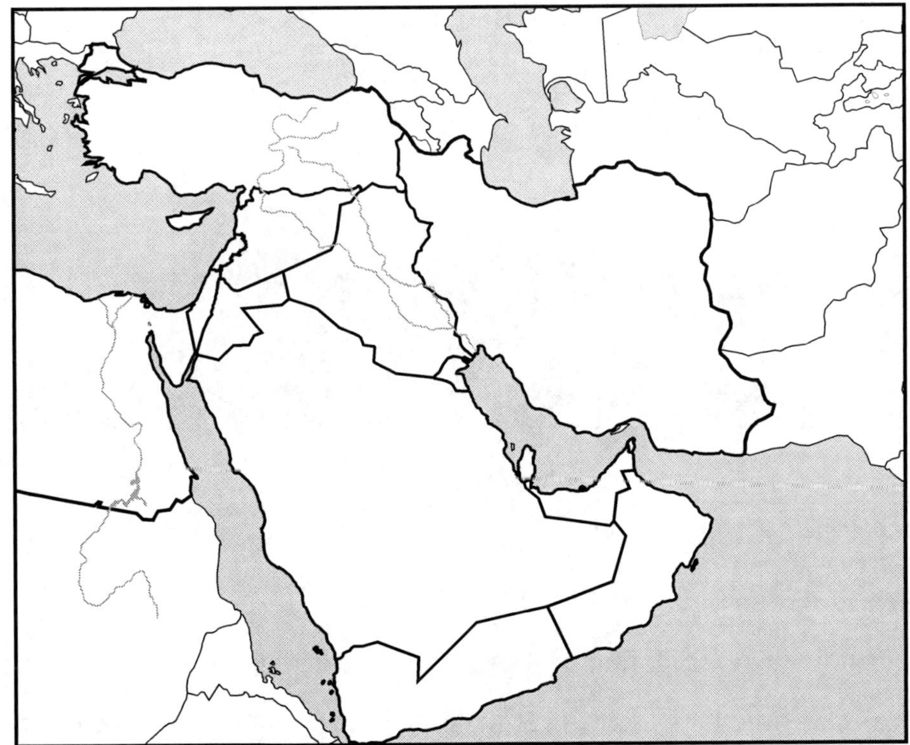

Using your map, describe the location of the Middle East relative to three other places.

____

____

UNIT 5 • ACTIVITY 66
Population: Israel and Saudi Arabia

Look at the population pyramids for Israel and Saudi Arabia below. Pay close attention to the population number in thousands or millions. Then answer the following questions on another sheet of paper.

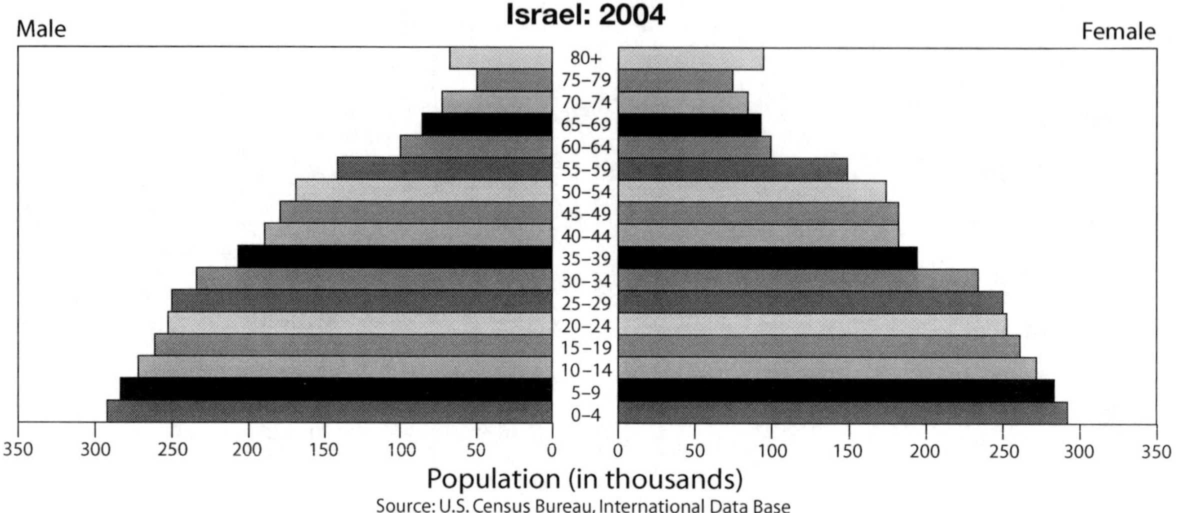

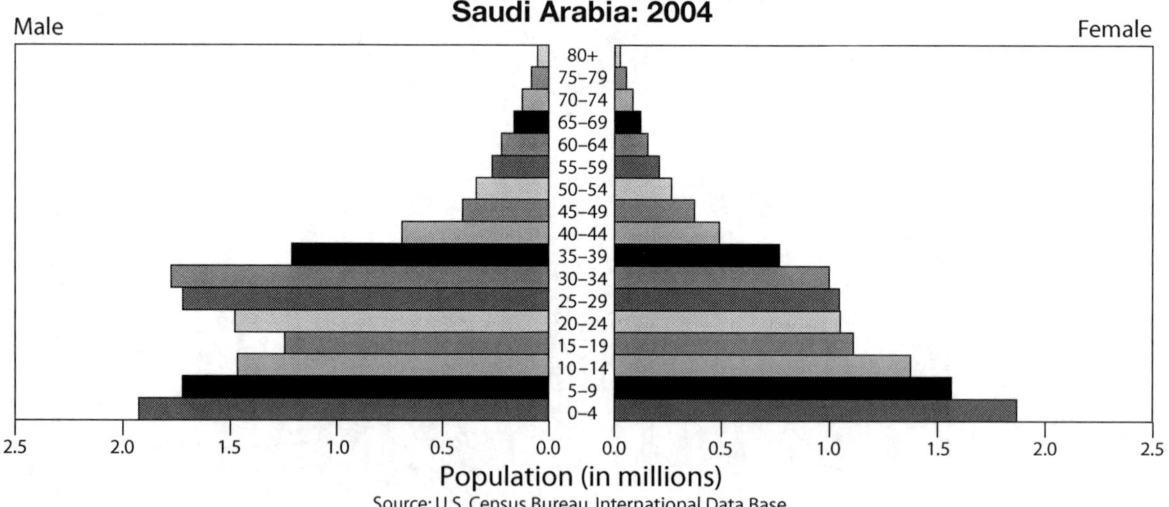

1. Which age group is the largest in both countries?
2. Both countries look as if they have experienced rapid growth. How do the pyramids show that?
3. Compare the number of females to males in each pyramid. Which country has a sharp difference between genders? (Remember, normal births tend to have relatively equal male/female ratios.) Speculate on the reasons why this might be the case.
4. Compare the life expectancy in these two countries. In which country do a larger percentage of the population live longer?

NAME:

UNIT 5 • ACTIVITY 67
Political Divisions in the Middle East

Use the clues below to complete the crossword puzzle.

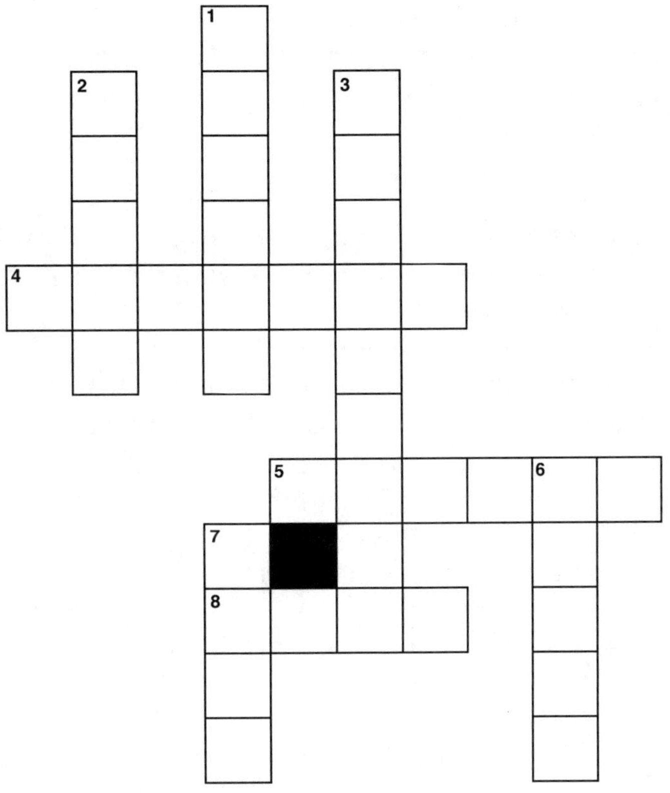

Across

4. This most densely populated country in the Middle East is smaller than New York City.
5. This most populated country in the Middle East straddles Europe and Asia.
8. The Tigris-Euphrates river system, birthplace of agriculture and early societies, is located mostly in the country of ____________.

Down

1. Since much of the Middle East is ____________, most population centers are along river systems.
2. Saudi Arabia is three times the size of which state in the United States?
3. The geographic area in which most Middle East countries are located is the Arabian ____________.
6. Although ____________ is on the continent of Africa, its culture and history place it within the Middle East.
7. Cairo, Egypt, is located along this river system.

NAME:

UNIT 5 • ACTIVITY 68
Global Chokepoints

A strait is a narrow body of water connecting two larger bodies of water. Global *chokepoints* are strategic straits or canals that could be closed or blocked to stop sea traffic. These waterways are often protected by international law. If they were not protected, a nearby country could close the waterway. This would harm global trade of important goods, such as petroleum. There are about 200 straits in the world, but only a few are considered chokepoints. Four of the eight listed below are in the Middle East.

Bab el Mandeb	This strait is located between the Red Sea and the Indian Ocean. Ships pass through to travel between the Mediterranean Sea and the Indian Ocean.
Bosporus and the Dardanelles	Control of these straits has for centuries been contested. The Russians wanted warm water access to the Mediterranean Sea. Today these straits are surrounded by Turkey and are considered international waters.
Gibraltar	This strait between the Mediterranean Sea and the Atlantic Ocean is protected by international treaty.
Panama Canal	Completed in 1914, this heavily used, 50-mile waterway cuts off an 8,000-mile trip from the East Coast of North America to the West Coast.
Strait of Hormuz	Iran and Iraq both placed mines in this area during the 1980s. This disrupted the transport of oil from the Persian Gulf to the Arabian Sea and on to the Indian Ocean.
Strait of Magellan	This strait, at the southern tip of South America, between the mainland and Tierra del Fuego, provides a shortcut that avoids traveling around Cape Horn.
Strait of Malacca	This strait in the Indian Ocean is used as a shortcut for oil exports from the Middle East to East Asia. Ships travel between Indonesia and Malaysia, which also have their own oil supplies.
Suez Canal	Built in 1869, this canal connects the Mediterranean Sea with the Red Sea. It remains a vulnerable target because of ongoing hostilities in the Middle East.

On another sheet of paper, write a paragraph to explain why these chokepoints should be protected by international laws. Provide at least three reasons to support your answer.

NAME:

UNIT 5 • ACTIVITY 69
The Euphrates

The Euphrates River is over 1,700 miles long. It is located in what was known in ancient history as Mesopotamia. This name means "between the rivers." The other river is the Tigris. Beginning in the Turkish highlands, the Euphrates runs through Syria and Iraq and empies into the Persian Gulf. Unpredictable flooding forced early cities in Mesopotamia to work together as communities. This led to dense population areas and classes. Now this flooding is prevented by dams and reservoirs. The river is navigable by shallow-draft boats. No heavy cargo or ocean freighters can pass. A 550-mile canal links the Tigris and the Euphrates.

Much controversy exists around the use of the river. Access to water means life or death for whole societies. In the Middle East, arid climates make conflict over water a most serious threat to peace in the region. The Euphrates is now the site of many dams and power plants in Turkey and Syria. This causes Iraqis to worry that there will not be enough water for their irrigation uses. Water pollution is an issue because of the Persian Gulf's oil resources. Rain that follows oil fires, accidental spills, and leakage washes pollution into the rivers. Dams prevent excess water from flowing through to dilute the pollution.

Use what you have learned from the information above and other resources to create a travel brochure. Your brochure should highlight the Euphrates River in a way that will make people want to visit. Do some research using reference books and web sites. Download pictures or make some drawings that show attractive features of the Euphrates and the areas it flows through. Include important sights along the river. Write the information for your brochure in clear, descriptive language. Use the space below to take notes or to design your brochure.

NAME: ______

UNIT 5 • ACTIVITY 70
All Deserts Are Not Equal

Read the information and the chart. Then answer the questions that follow.

A *desert* is an area of land that receives less than 10 inches of rainfall a year. One third of Earth's land area is covered by desert. This area is increasing because of desertification at a rate of 80,000 miles every year.

Sub-tropical deserts are the hottest. They are dry areas with rapid evaporation.

Cool coastal deserts are cooler because cold ocean currents prevent rain clouds from forming over the nearby land.

Cold winter deserts experience temperature extremes between seasons, ranging from 100 degrees F in summer to 10 degrees F in winter.

The polar regions are considered deserts since nearly all their moisture is contained in ice.

Desert	Location	Type of Desert	Area (square miles)	Facts
Sahara	northern Africa	sub-tropical	3.5 million sq. m.	Only 30% sand
Arabian	Arabian Peninsula	sub-tropical	1 million sq. m.	world's largest stretch of unbroken sand
Kalahari	southern Africa	sub-tropical	220,000 sq. m.	sand sheets
Great Western	Australia	sub-tropical	520,000 sq. m.	Gibson, Great Sandy, and Great Victoria are part of this Outback
Atacama	Chile	cool coastal	54,000 sq. m.	world's driest desert; salt, lava, sand
Great Basin	western parts of the U.S.	cold winter	190,000 sq. m.	mountain ridges, valleys, 1% sand dunes
Patagonian	Argentina	cold winter	260,000 sq. m.	gravel plains, plateaus, basalt sheets
Kara Kum	Uzbekistan, Turkmenistan	cold winter	135,000 sq.m.	90% gray layered sand
Gobi	China, Mongolia	cold winter	500,000 sq. m.	stony, sandy soil: steppes (dry grasslands)
Antarctic	Antarctica	polar	5.4 million sq. m.	ice, snow, bedrock

1. What is the largest nonpolar desert? ______
2. Which desert is on the coast next to cold ocean currents? ______
3. Agree or disagree with this statement: "All deserts are sandy." Support your answer with three examples. ______
4. Write your own question using the information above. ______

______

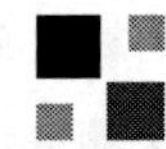

NAME: ____________________

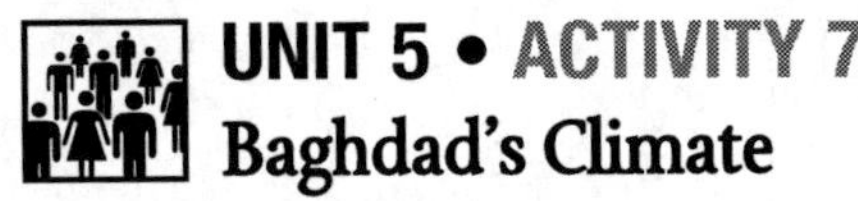

UNIT 5 • ACTIVITY 71
Baghdad's Climate

Create a climograph by plotting the precipitation and temperature from the chart below. Then answer the questions on another sheet of paper.

Baghdad, Iraq, is at about 33° 22' N 44° 30' E.
Average Temperature and Precipitation

	Jan	Feb	Mar	Apr	May	Jun	Jul	Aug	Sep	Oct	Nov	Dec	Year
°F	48.9	53.2	61.2	70.9	81.9	90.1	94.3	93.6	87.4	76.8	63.0	52.0	72.8
inches	1.1	1.1	1.1	0.7	0.3	0.0	0.0	0.0	0.0	0.1	0.8	1.0	6.2

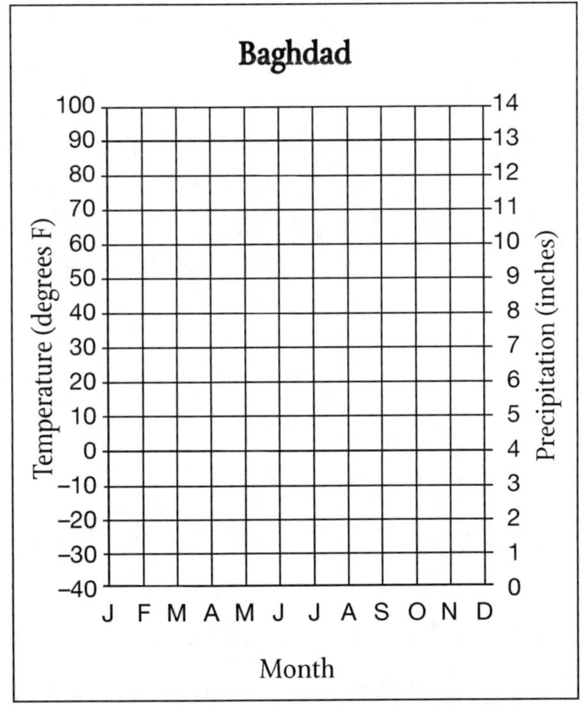

1. Look at the average precipitation. What conclusions can you reach about the local geography here? ____________________

____

2. Will local farmers be able to rely on regular rainfall, or will irrigation be necessary? ____________________

____

3. What is the difference in degrees between the coldest and warmest months? ____________________

4. Create a question of your own based on the climograph. ____________________

____

NAME:

UNIT 5 • ACTIVITY 72
Irrigation

Read the paragraphs below. Then answer the questions that follow.

Irrigation is the watering of dry land by artificial means. Today, over 18% of all cropland in the world is irrigated in order to meet the global food demand. There are many methods of irrigation. Early Egyptians built canals and dams using animal power to help irrigate crops. This method is still used in rural Egypt today. The ancient Chinese created methods of getting water to rice crops that did not depend on rain or natural flooding. Farmers in the Americas also developed ways of irrigating their crops. Now reservoirs, tanks, wells, canals, and pipelines get water to a field. There, several methods are used to supply it. These include flooding, channeling water in streams between rows, spraying water through large sprinklers, or using drip irrigation. Drip irrigation is a slow, drop-by-drop application of water just above the soil surface. This reduces evaporation and water waste.

Israel is a good example of how people have harnessed technology to improve agriculture. Israel has a desertlike climate with little freshwater or farmland. The Israeli government has built the Israeli National Water Carrier, which carries water from the Sea of Galilee. The water is desalinated (salt is removed) and then used in drip irrigation in the Negev desert. Crops include potatoes, apples, bananas, avocados, and cotton. Israel produces enough food for its own population and even exports crops. In the future, it may be possible to use Ice Age water deposits deep below the desert to supply Israel with water. Water is precious, so conservation efforts in farming are widely supported by Israelis.

1. What is irrigation? ____________________

____

2. As a farmer in Israel, why would you welcome the government's investment in drip irrigation?

____

____

3. What are some of the crops grown in Israel on drip-irrigated land? ____________________

____

4. Water is often taken for granted. What would it be like to live where water was a scarce resource? ____________________

____

____

5. Some scientists argue that widespread use of irrigation will use up water supplies and bring too much salt into the soil, making it unusable for farming. In your opinion, should deserts be made into farmland? On another sheet of paper, write your response in a well-thought-out paragraph.

NAME:

UNIT 5 • ACTIVITY 73
OPEC

Read the paragraph below. Then answer the questions that follow.

The Organization of Petroleum Exporting Countries (OPEC) includes countries that have joined together to talk about the production, pricing, and drilling of oil. The organization was founded in 1960 at a Baghdad conference. It is headquartered in Vienna, Austria. The members agree on the quantity and prices of the oil exported around the world. Member countries hold about 75% of the world's oil reserves (oil that geologists say is still in the ground but has not yet been drilled). OPEC members supply about 40% of the world's oil.

OPEC Members:

Algeria, Indonesia, Iran, Iraq, Kuwait, Libya, Nigeria, Qatar, Saudi Arabia, United Arab Emirates, Venezuela

Major non-OPEC oil-producing nations:

Canada, Mexico, Norway, Oman, Russia, United States

1. Looking at a map of the world, answer this question: Which nations in OPEC are in the Middle East?

____

2. How many oil-producing nations are not in the Middle East? ______________________________

____

3. Why do you think that wars are fought over oil? ______________________________

____

____

4. What suggestions do you have to reduce U.S. reliance on foreign oil? ______________________________

____

____

____

____

NAME:

UNIT 6 • ACTIVITY 74
Population in Dominoes

Look at the chart below. Then answer the questions.

Population density = number of people per square mile. The higher the number, the more people live close together.

Place	United States	China	Philippines	Singapore	Bangladesh	India	Mongolia	Taiwan	Japan
Population Density	75	327	625	17,702	2,254	856	4	13,887	875

Numbers mean nothing unless you make the numbers come alive. For example, there are 6.4 billion people on Earth. If a billion people were spaced 15 inches apart, they would form a straight line from Earth to the moon.

Now use dominoes as visual aids. Imagine that the dominoes below represent one square mile. For every ten people per square mile, imagine you are stacking one domino on top of another. On top of the United States rectangle, there will be 7.5 dominoes. Figure how many dominoes you will need to stack on each of the others. Write your answers on the dominoes.

1. What do these domino stacks represent? ______________________________
2. How many dominoes are stacked in Singapore? ____________
3. How would you explain population density to a younger person? Make the numbers friendly.

____

____

United States

China

Philippines

Singapore

Bangladesh

India

Mongolia

Taiwan

Japan

NAME:

UNIT 6 • ACTIVITY 75
Population: China and Bangladesh

Use the data below to fill in the two modified population pyramids—one for China and one for Bangladesh. Then, on another sheet of paper, answer the questions that follow.

Males % of pop.	0–19	20–39	40–59	60+	Females % of pop.	0–19	20–39	40–59	60+
China	17	18	11	5	China	16	17	11	5
Bangladesh	25	16	8	3	Bangladesh	23	16	7	3

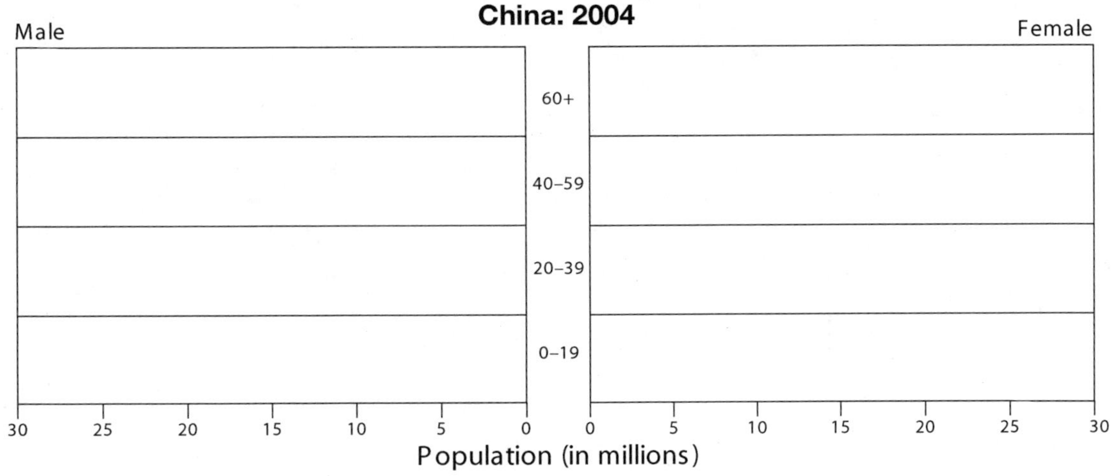

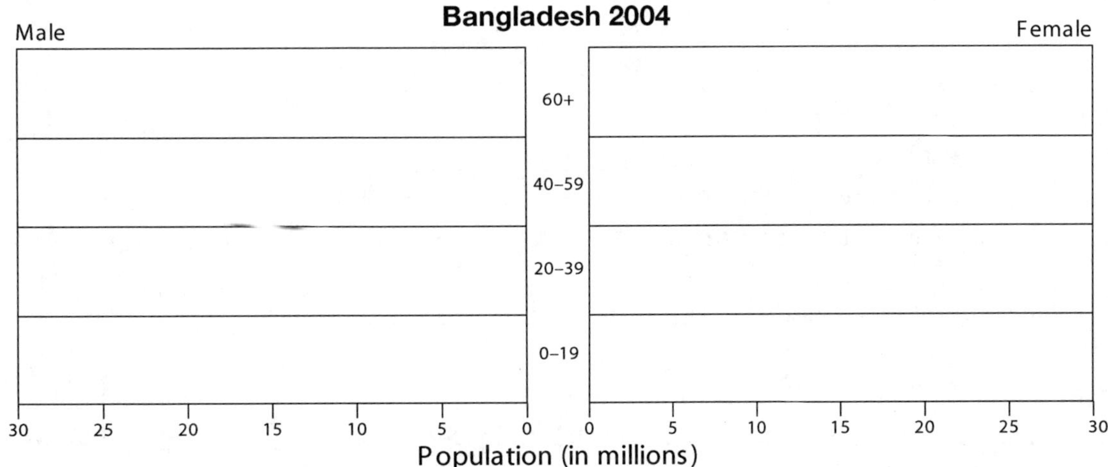

1. What type of growth rate is each nation experiencing? (slow, rapid, negative)
2. In which country are almost half the people under the age of 20?
3. Compare life expectancy in the two countries.

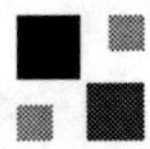

NAME:

UNIT 6 • ACTIVITY 76
Political Divisions in Asia

Use the clues to complete the crossword puzzle.

Across

1. The largest nation entirely in Asia is ____________.
5. Bangladesh and Pakistan are north of the large country of ____________.
6. A large part of a larger landmass that is somewhat separate from the landmass is called a ____________.
7. This peninsula is divided at the 38th parallel into two countries.

Down

2. Malaysia, Singapore, Indonesia, and the Philippines are all ____________ nations in Southeast Asia.
3. Afghanistan and Nepal are both ____________ countries in South Asia, since they do not border any sea water.
4. Japan is an ____________ nation, composed of over 10,000 islands.
6. Tibet has autonomous rule within China, which means it has limited power to ____________ -govern.

NAME: ______________________________

UNIT 6 • ACTIVITY 77
Archipelagos

Read the paragraphs below. Then answer the questions that follow.

Archipelagos

An *archipelago* is a set of closely clustered islands in any large body of water. They are often volcanic, forming along the ocean plate boundaries or hot spots in the ocean floor. Many times some of the islands in the chain are much older than others. One example is the Galápagos. One of the islands is four million years old and another is just forming due to volcanic action beneath it.

The largest archipelago is Indonesia, which has 18,103 islands in its chain. About 6,000 of those islands are populated. Indonesia stretches over 3,300 miles (similar to the area of the United States from California to Bermuda). Japan has over 3,000 islands. Other archipelagos are smaller. Hawaii has only 137 islands, and the Galápagos has 13. There are almost 70 archipelagos worldwide, some of which are independent nations and others that are part of a larger island or country. There is even a company in Dubai (United Arab Emirates) that is constructing an archipelago of artificial islands. These will be private islands, resorts, and estates for the wealthy. The name of their archipelago is "The World," since the islands are placed to look from the air like the continents of Earth.

1. What is an archipelago? ______________________________

   ____

2. Why do island chains form like this over time? ______________________________

   ____

3. What occupations do you imagine the people living on these island nations engage in?

   ____

   ____

4. What do you think would be some of the challenges of governing an archipelago nation that is spread out? ______________________________

   ____

   ____

5. On another sheet of paper, design your own archipelago. What would be the purpose of your island chain? Explain below.

   ____

   ____

   ____

   ____

NAME:

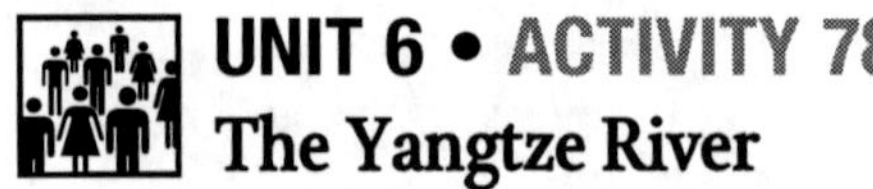

UNIT 6 • ACTIVITY 78
The Yangtze River

The Yangtze River is the longest river in Asia and, at 3,900 miles, the third longest in the world. It is an immensely important and largely navigable river. It is known in Chinese as Chang Jiang, meaning "Long River." From its source in the Tibetan Plateau to the East China Sea, the river drains over 695,000 square miles of land. Over 350 million people live along its banks (more people than live in the entire United States). Important cities along its banks include Shanghai, the "gateway" to the Yangtze. Thousands of boats crowd the harbor here. Nanking is also a major city along the Yangtze. The river is considered the lifeline of China since so much trade passes along it.

The Three Gorges Dam Project is China's largest construction project since the Great Wall. It will eventually create the world's largest hydroelectric power plant. It will also increase the ability of freighters to navigate into the interior of China. It will create farming and industrial possibilities. The government of China also argues that the construction of the dam will prevent thousands from dying during unexpected flooding. When the dam began construction, however, 1.5 million people were resettled. Their villages were flooded. Archeological sites were also flooded. Some environmentalists are concerned about the effect the dam will have on local animal species, including the baiji dolphin, river sturgeon, and finless porpoises. They are all protected wildlife. Construction of the dam is expected to be completed in 2009.

You have been invited to participate in a "parade of rivers." Your task is to use what you have learned from the information above to create a sketch of a parade float that highlights the Yangtze River. Include on your float the physical type of geographic area that the river runs through. Your float might include signs with the names of large cities along the river, any threats the river basin area faces, a symbol you design, or a slogan you write that sums up your sketch.

NAME:

UNIT 6 • ACTIVITY 79
Ring of Fire

Use the paragraph and the map below to answer the questions that follow.

The Ring of Fire is the name used to describe the active volcanic zone that circles the Pacific Basin. It stretches from New Zealand, along the eastern edge of Asia, north across the Aleutian islands of Alaska, and south along the coast of North and South America. It is composed of over 75% of the world's active and dormant volcanoes. Geologists have confirmed that Earth's crust is made up of over 12 continental sheets or plates. These plates move very slowly across the surface of Earth, occasionally bumping into one another, causing seismic activity at the borders of the plates—especially around the Ring of Fire. This can cause earthquakes, volcanic eruptions, and tsunamis.

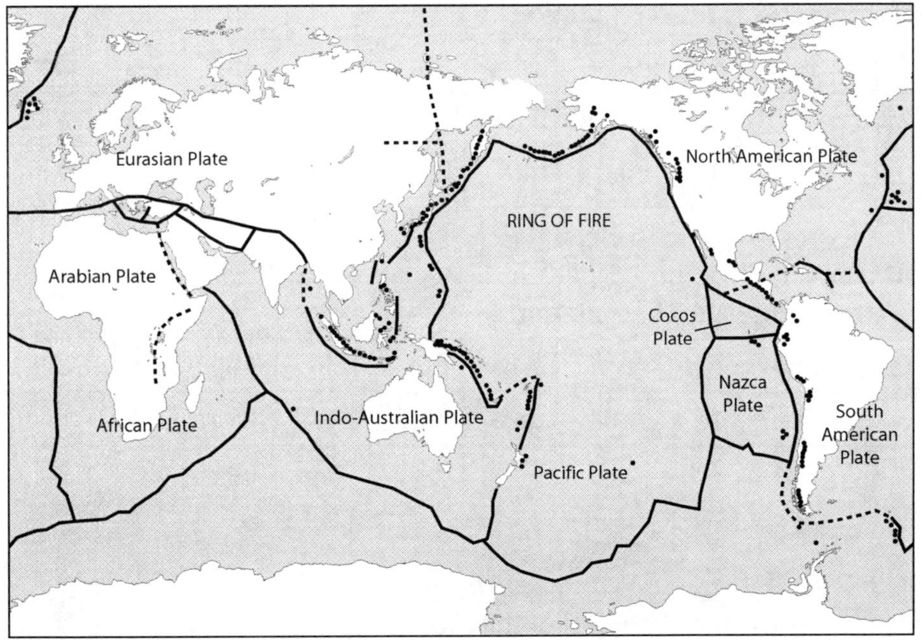

1. How do you think the Ring of Fire got its name? ______________________________

2. What are the three plates that border or include Asia? ______________________________

____

3. The small circles on the map represent active volcanoes. Where are most of them located?

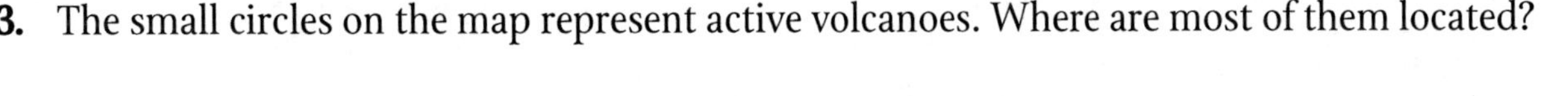

____

4. The Pacific Ocean is growing at the rate of 1–2 inches a year. Why does this make sense when you look at the map showing the number of plate borders in the Pacific Ocean region?

____

NAME:

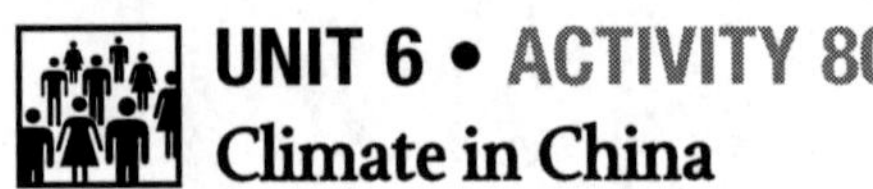

UNIT 6 • ACTIVITY 80
Climate in China

On another sheet of paper, create a climograph for each city below. Then answer the questions.

Harbin, China, is at about 45° 45' N 126° 41' E.
Average Temperature and Precipitation

	Jan	Feb	Mar	Apr	May	Jun	Jul	Aug	Sep	Oct	Nov	Dec	Year
°F	–3.2	4.3	22.6	42.8	57.4	67.6	73.4	70.3	57.7	42.1	21.0	3.2	38.3
inches	0.2	0.2	0.4	0.9	1.7	3.5	6.1	4.6	2.4	1.1	0.4	0.2	21.7

Lhasa (Tibet), China, is at about 29° 40' N 91° 9' E.
Average Temperature and Precipitation

	Jan	Feb	Mar	Apr	May	Jun	Jul	Aug	Sep	Oct	Nov	Dec	Year
°F	29.1	34.2	40.6	47.1	54.3	60.8	59.9	58.5	55.6	47.3	36.7	30.0	46.2
inches	0.0	0.1	0.1	0.2	0.9	2.8	5.2	5.0	2.3	0.4	0.1	0.0	17.1

Shanghai, China, is at about 31° 14' N 121° 28' E.
Average Temperature and Precipitation

	Jan	Feb	Mar	Apr	May	Jun	Jul	Aug	Sep	Oct	Nov	Dec	Year
°F	37.9	39.7	46.8	56.7	65.8	73.6	81.3	81.1	73.8	63.9	53.1	43.0	59.7
inches	1.8	2.4	3.3	3.7	4.1	6.8	5.7	5.4	5.4	2.7	2.1	1.5	44.9

1. Which city is the most tropical of the three? ______________________

2. In which city does altitude prevent higher temperature? ______________________

3. Which city gets the coldest? ______________________

4. What other facts about these cities can you determine from the climographs you made?

____

____

NAME:

UNIT 6 • ACTIVITY 81
Rice

Read the paragraph. Then answer the questions that follow.

Asia grows and consumes 90% of the world's rice crop. China produces more rice than any other country. Yet East Asia does not have a wealth of arable land, so people use terracing to make good use of the space. Much of China's rice production is in the south, where there is rich alluvial (fertile river) soil. Second in world rice production, India also has plentiful rain, a long growing season, and good alluvial soil. Rice is Japan's main crop, which it produces mostly for its own needs. The Japanese, too, must use terracing to get a high yield per acre.

The four largest exporters of rice include Thailand, the United States, Vietnam, and China. Rice is grown in the United States in areas that must be heavily irrigated because of arid (dry) climates. This practice has been controversial. There is some question whether farmers should be growing rice in desertlike climates, draining off needed water from people downstream.

The process of rice growing differs somewhat from place to place. In some areas, it is lengthy and involves the whole family and community. For example, in Indonesia, the following steps are followed. The field (paddy) is first prepared by the men with hoes, breaking up the soil. The field is then leveled by animal and human labor to make a smooth bed, making sure the water is level. One at a time, the rice seedlings are transplanted by the women workers. Men place fertilizer on the young plants and then weed them, allowing the weeds to act as fertilizer. After the rice grows, the women harvest it by cutting each stalk individually and then threshing the rice (taking the stalks and husks off of it). The rice is then dried. Next, it is pounded to take off the hull, or to make rice flour. The rice can then be cooked and eaten, stored, or sold at market.

1. How would you compare rice-growing conditions in China, India, and Japan? ______________

   ____

2. What is the secret to successful rice farming? ______________________

   ____

3. Describe the process by which rice is grown in Indonesia. Why is it described as a labor-intensive crop? ______________________

   ____

   ____

4. Research rice growing in California. Compare the process in California with the process in Indonesia. Write your findings on another sheet of papaer.

NAME:

UNIT 6 • ACTIVITY 82
The Tokyo Fish Market

A trip to Japan would not be complete without a trip to Tokyo's Tsukiji fish market. One of Japan's major industries is fishing, and this shows in the sheer size of the Tokyo market.

Tsukiji is not the early-morning destination only for the best sushi chefs, restaurateurs, and merchants. It also attracts tourists who want to see the excitement of the market and watch the fish auctions. Huge tuna, which have been flash frozen far out at sea, and other marine products are sold to the highest bidder. In addition, row upon row of fish vendors market their wares, getting spectators to sample and buy their fresh morning catch. Over 2,800 tons of fish are sold here each day, 780,000 tons a year.

Imagine what it is like to work as an owner of one of the hundreds of stalls in the fish market. Create a slogan and an advertising poster for one of the fish merchants to use at the market. You might consider reaching not only the local Japanese customers, but also the tourists who are walking through the market.

NAME:

UNIT 6 • ACTIVITY 83
Dams

The Facts About Dams

The building of large dams in the world today is very controversial, yet there are 40,000 large dams in the world and over 300 major dams.

The World Commission on Dams is an independent organization formed under the World Bank to look at the good and bad effects of dam building worldwide. The commission released their report in 2000. Many in the World Bank and in the dam industry feel that they have been betrayed, since the report was not favorable toward large dam projects.

The World Commission on Dams claimed in its report that

- Poor people are the ones forced to move as large dams are built and their villages flooded. These people are rarely given any money to relocate and find new jobs.
- The release of greenhouse (methane) gases as vegetation-rich water evaporates in reservoirs contributes to global warming.
- Many fish species become extinct because they cannot make it past the dams, despite fish ladders built for that purpose.
- Farmlands become less fertile because natural regular flooding of rivers no longer occurs.
- Archeological sites are often lost as areas are flooded.

Hydroelectric companies and dam supporters argue that

- Electricity generated by power projects is a clean source of fuel.
- Dams (and the reservoirs that are behind them) provide recreational areas for boating and fishing.
- Large projects provide employment for local people and fuel the local economy.
- People who have been forced to relocate have been compensated.
- Fish ladders have been built that help to preserve the river system and its inhabitants.

On another sheet of paper, write a letter to the World Commission on Dams sharing your opinion about dam building.

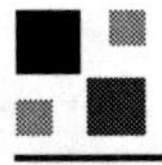

NAME:

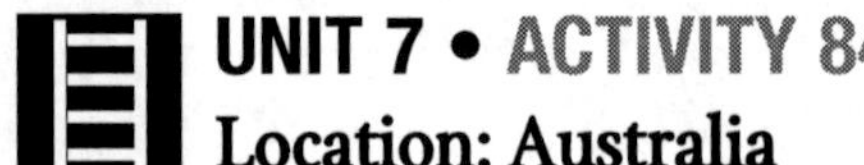

UNIT 7 • ACTIVITY 84
Location: Australia

During the late 1700s, Europeans arrived in Oceania and Australia. They first came to Australia and New Zealand and then the Pacific Ocean islands. At that time, there were more than 300,000 aboriginal people living in Australia alone. Disease, relocation, and conflict reduced that number greatly. The wildlife and plants that were native to the area were unique because they were so far away from other land. That is why there are no wild kangaroos, koalas, kookaburras, or platypuses anywhere else in the world.

Once European explorers arrived, Australia quickly became populated with European immigrants, including convicts from the British Isles. Australia became the home of an increasing number of Asian immigrants in the twentieth century. Air travel, satellites, and telecommunications have ended the isolation of this area. There are still distant cities (Perth is more than 1,400 miles away from the next major city). Remote places still exist where you can almost imagine what Australia looked like before Europeans came.

Label the places below on the map. The list shows the distance between Sydney, Australia, (33° S 151° E) and each city.

3,900 miles away from Singapore (1° N 103° E)

5,000 miles away from Tokyo, Japan (35° N 139° E)

5,100 miles from Honolulu, Hawaii (21° N 157° W)

7,200 miles from Buenos Aires, Argentina (34° S 58° W)

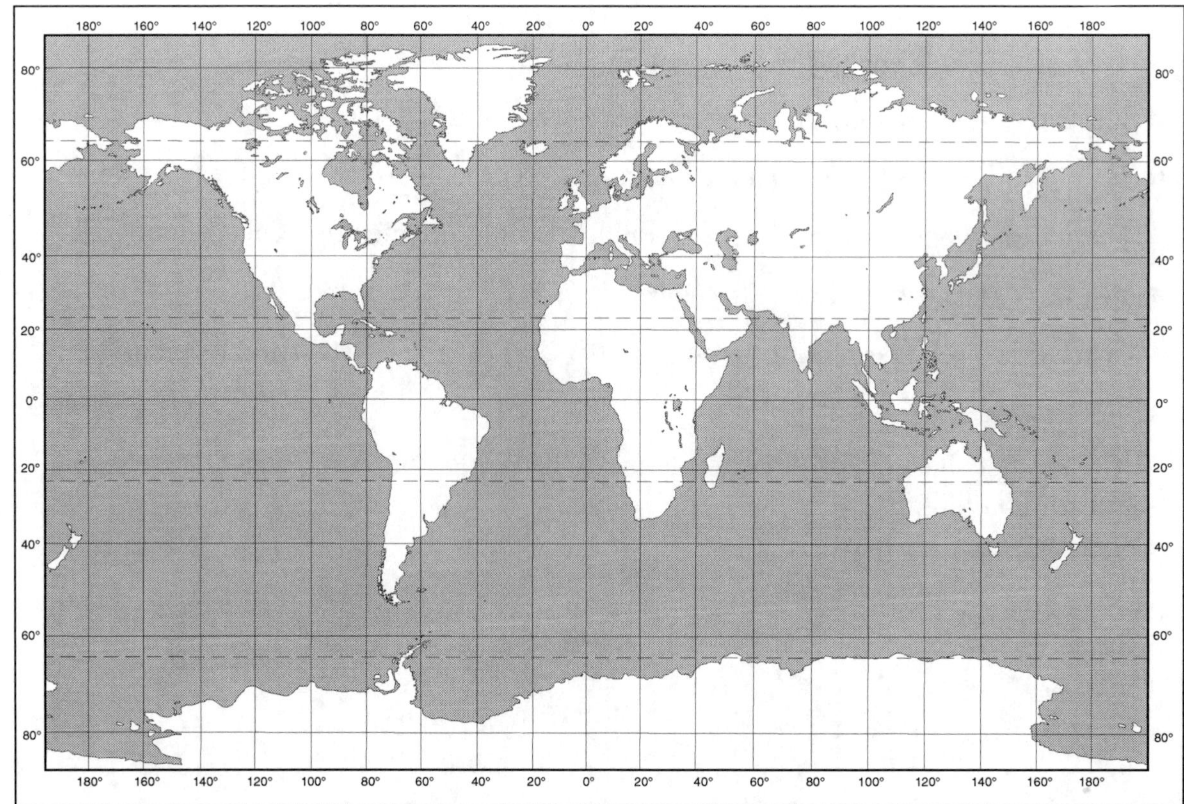

NAME:

UNIT 7 • ACTIVITY 85
Population: New Zealand

Look at the population pyramid for New Zealand. Then answer the questions that follow. Pay close attention to the population number in thousands.

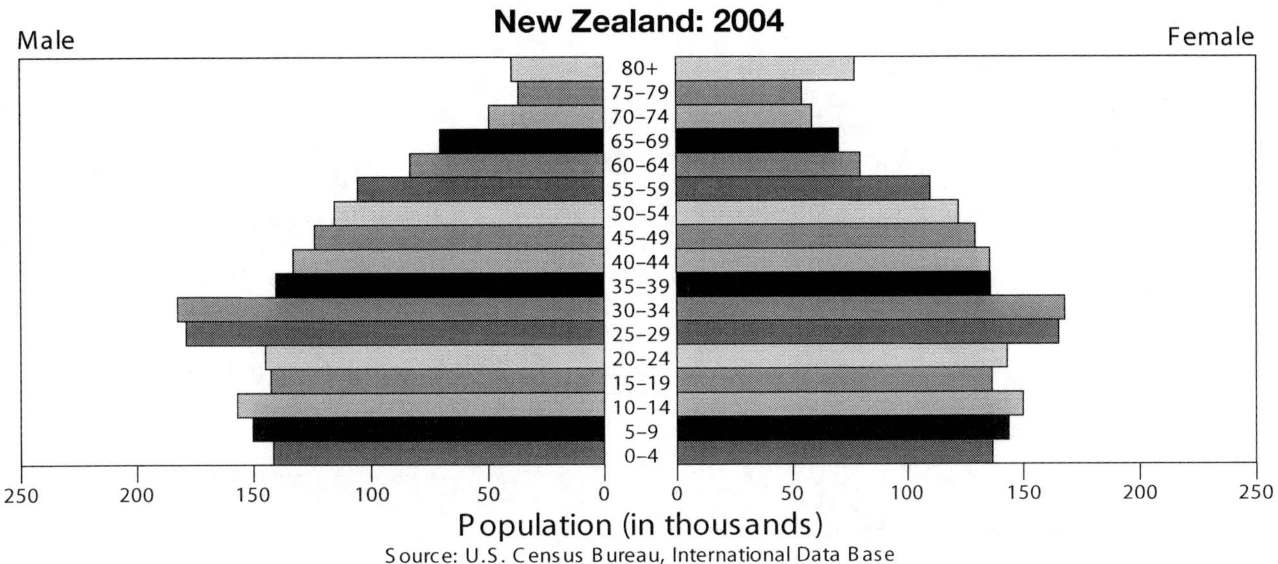

1. Who tends to live longer in New Zealand—men or women? ______________________

2. Were there more boys ages 0–4 in 2004 in New Zealand or more girls? ____________

3. At what age range do females begin to outnumber males? ____________

4. What age range makes up the largest group in New Zealand? ______________________

5. Compare the number of males who are 0–4 years old with the number that are 35–39. ________

____

6. Explain why this population pyramid shows slow growth. ______________________

____

NAME:

UNIT 7 • ACTIVITY 86
Water, Oceania, and Australia

Use the clues to complete the crossword puzzle.

						1				2					
				3		4									
										5					
			6												
	7														
			8												

Across

4. The island of Tasmania is across the _______________ Strait from Australia.
5. A ring-shaped coral island surrounding a lagoon is called a(n) _______________.
6. About 95% of people in _______________ live within 100 miles of the coast.
7. The Australian term for hurricanes is _______________.
8. The islands of Oceania are spread across this ocean.

Down

1. This is the largest coral reef in the world. (3 words)
2. This is a country composed of a string of volcanic mountains spread over two main islands.
3. Australia's nickname is _______________.

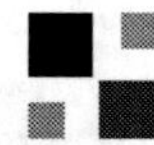

NAME:

UNIT 7 • ACTIVITY 87

The Murray River

Mark Twain compared the Murray River to the Mississippi River when he visited Australia in the late 1800s. Even though the Murray is much smaller, it helped explorers map out Australia. Later, the river helped with trade and communication. The river flows 1,572 miles, beginning in the Snowy Mountains and emptying into the Southern Ocean. Most of it is navigable. Hundreds of paddle steamboats traveled up and down the river in the 1880s. They carried passengers and goods such as wool and wheat. Trade is now mostly handled by rail, plane, and highways. Droughts and flooding initially made travel dangerous. The river is now controlled through a series of locks. These help manage the river flow. Today, the river is used for many recreational activities, including boating and fishing. There are also national parks alongside it. Thanks to irrigation, orchards and vineyards could be planted along its banks. Tourists visit historic towns and view the abundant wildlife as they travel down the river.

You have been invited to participate in a "parade of rivers." Your task is to use what you have learned from the information above to create a sketch below of a parade float that highlights the Murray River. Include on your float the physical type of geographic area that the river runs through. Your float might include signs with the names of large cities along the river, any threats the river basin area faces, a symbol you design, or a slogan you write that sums up your sketch.

NAME:

UNIT 7 • ACTIVITY 88
A Mysterious Place in Australia

You have been selected to guess the mystery place.

Use the hints below to help you figure it out. Use reference books and atlases, if necessary. Write the names of the mystery place.

1. It is located on an island continent that is the least mountainous in the world.
2. It was once in the middle of an inland ocean floor, but it now stands 1,100 feet above sea level.
3. It is over 6 miles in circumference.
4. It is located in the middle of a desert.
5. It is a sacred site to aboriginal peoples, being central to beliefs about dreamtime.
6. The site is owned and managed by aboriginal peoples.
7. Photographers love to watch it change colors as different natural light plays over it.

   The name of the mystery place is ______________________________,

   but it is better known as ______________________________.

NAME: ______

UNIT 7 • ACTIVITY 89
Climate in Australia

On another sheet of paper, create a climograph for each city below. Then answer the questions.

Melbourne, Australia, is at about 37° 50' S 144° 58' E.
Average Temperature and Precipitation

	Jan	Feb	Mar	Apr	May	Jun	Jul	Aug	Sep	Oct	Nov	Dec	Year
°F	67.8	67.8	64.9	59.5	54.3	50.4	49.1	51.1	54.3	57.9	61.3	65.1	58.6
inches	1.9	1.9	2.1	2.3	2.3	1.9	1.9	2.0	2.3	2.6	2.4	2.3	25.9

Alice Springs, Australia, is at about 23° 42' N 133° 53' E.
Average Temperature and Precipitation

	Jan	Feb	Mar	Apr	May	Jun	Jul	Aug	Sep	Oct	Nov	Dec	Year
°F	83.3	81.9	76.6	68.0	59.9	54.1	52.7	57.7	64.9	72.9	78.3	81.9	69.4
inches	1.6	1.6	1.4	0.7	0.7	0.7	0.5	0.4	0.4	0.8	1.0	1.5	11.3

Darwin, Australia, is at about 12° 28' N 130° 50' E.
Average Temperature and Precipitation

	Jan	Feb	Mar	Apr	May	Jun	Jul	Aug	Sep	Oct	Nov	Dec	Year
°F	83.3	82.8	83.1	83.5	81.1	78.1	76.8	78.8	82.2	84.6	85.1	84.6	82.0
inches	15.6	13.0	11.1	3.8	0.7	0.1	0.0	0.1	0.6	2.4	5.1	9.4	61.9

1. When is the rainy season in Darwin? ______

2. What is the difference in annual precipitation between Alice Springs and Darwin? ______

______

3. Looking at the three climographs, how can you tell Australia is located in the Southern Hemisphere? ______

______

4. Create a question of your own based on the climographs. ______

______

______

NAME:

UNIT 7 • ACTIVITY 90
A Country of Sheep

Read the passage below, and then draw a cartoon or a visual that shows the relationship between sheep and people in New Zealand.

Ratio of Sheep to People—20 : 1

The first sheep arrived in New Zealand with Captain Cook in 1773. By 1982, there were 70 million sheep on the island. This translated to 20 sheep for every resident of New Zealand. The number is now somewhat lower due to declining profits in the sheep industry. New Zealand is a leading exporter of wool, exporting mainly to Asia. New Zealand also exports frozen lamb and mutton across the globe. Australia also has a large sheep industry which, during its boom in the 1830s, was responsible for forcing the native population to move from valuable grazing land.

NAME:

UNIT 7 • ACTIVITY 91
Thinking About Energy Sources

In Oceania, particularly Australia and New Zealand, energy resources have been an important trade good. Australia is the third largest producer of coal (at 7.5%). Note, though, that China and the United States combined produce 55% of the world total. Petroleum has also been an energy resource of significance. New Zealand is the 25th largest producer at .13%.

Study the chart below, and answer the questions that follow.

Petroleum Production and Consumption Comparison
% of total world production/consumption, based on 2003 statistics
Statistical Review of World Energy 2004

Country	Oil Production	Oil Consumption
Saudi Arabia	12.84%	1.84%
Russian Federation	11.40%	3.43 %
United States	9.23%	25.14%
Iran	5.14%	1.48%
Mexico	5.11%	2.27%
China	4.58%	7.57%
Venezuela	4.15%	.66%
Norway	4.14%	.26%
Canada	3.84%	2.65%
United Arab Emirates	3.19%	.41%
Australia	.72%	1.05%

1. What percentage of the world's oil supply does the United States consume? ________________
   What percentage of the world's oil supply does the U.S. produce? ________________
   Where does the U.S. get the oil that it does not produce at home? ________________
2. Note that the next highest country in consumption is China. What does the fact that the United States uses a much higher percentage of world oil say about the type of society in which U.S. residents live?

   ____
3. Compare Australia's production and consumption with Venezuela's, and China's with Mexico's.

   ____
4. What are the only three countries listed here that import oil, since they use more than they produce? ____

NAME:

UNIT 7 • ACTIVITY 92
Antarctica: Honoring Explorers

Look at the names of places, landforms, ice forms, and bodies of water on a map of Antarctica. Many of the geographic features are named after people associated with Antarctica and its explorers. Do some research and then, on another sheet of paper, write brief accounts of the people honored by the following Antarctic names. Use the line after each name to record your source or sources of information about that feature.

Alexander Island ______________________________

Axel Heiberg Glacier ______________________________

Beardmore Glacier ______________________________

Cape Agassiz ______________________________

Ellsworth Land and Mountains ______________________________

Filcher Ice Shelf ______________________________

Ingrid Christensen Coast ______________________________

Lambert Glacier ______________________________

Marie Byrd Land ______________________________

Queen Maud Land ______________________________

Rockefeller Plateau ______________________________

Ronne Ice Shelf ______________________________

Ross Ice Shelf, Island, and Sea ______________________________

Shackleton Ice Shelf ______________________________

Vinson Massif ______________________________

Weddell Sea ______________________________

NAME:

UNIT 7 • ACTIVITY 93
Two Polar Expeditions

Use words from the box to fill in the missing parts of the story.

Axel Heiberg Glacier	South Polar Plateau	Ross Sea
blizzard	Beardmore Glacier	South Pole
Ross Island	Ross Ice Shelf	

In 1911, two groups raced each other to be the first people to reach the **1.** ______________________, the extreme southern end of the earth. Roald Amundsen led a group from Norway. Robert Scott led a group from England. Both set up base camps next to the **2.** ______________________, an indentation in the southern coast of Antarctica. Scott's camp was on **3.** ______________________, which shared its name with the neighboring sea and ice shelf.

Leaving base camp, each expedition first crossed the **4.** ______________________, a huge slab of floating ice. Amundsen's group started on October 19, two weeks earlier than Ross's group did. Amundsen and his men then had to climb the **5.** ______________________, a high, packed mass of ice. At the top, the vast, gently rolling **6.** ______________________ stretched out to the pole. The Amundsen group reached the pole on December 14, 1911.

Ross and his men, meanwhile, struggled to cross the high, icy **7.** ______________________ to the east of Amundsen's route. They reached the pole on January 17, only to find the flag of Norway there before them. A fierce, raging Antarctic **8.** ______________________ trapped Ross and his men on their return trip from the pole. Sadly, all members of the group died.

NAME: ______________________________

UNIT 7 • ACTIVITY 94
Climate in Antarctica

In recent years, scientists have observed and recorded a number of instances of ice shelf calving in Antarctica. Calving occurs when chunks of ice shelves and glaciers break off and become icebergs—great, floating masses of ice. Calving is a normal process for ice shelves and glaciers. But some observers think this recent amount of calving activity—even ice shelf collapse—is related to higher temperatures possibly caused by global warming. What do you think?

First, on a large map of Antarctica, draw boundary lines to show the changes in the ice shelves listed below due to various calving events in the 1990s and 2000s. Or, you could find and print out Internet images of these changes.

- Larsen Ice Shelf
- Ronne-Filcher Ice Shelf
- Ross Ice Shelf

Now, answer these questions about ONE of these ice shelves.

1. How much area, in square miles, has this ice shelf lost since 1995? ______________________

2. Which U.S. state's or states' area does this lost Antarctic area equal or exceed? Give the name of the state or states and its or their total square miles. ______________________

____

3. What has happened so far to the icebergs calved from this ice shelf?

____

____

____

4. What reasons do different scientists suggest for these changes in the Antarctic ice shelves?

____

____

____

____

5. In your opinion, what is causing these ice shelf changes?

____

____

____